STEEPED
IN THE WORLD OF TEA

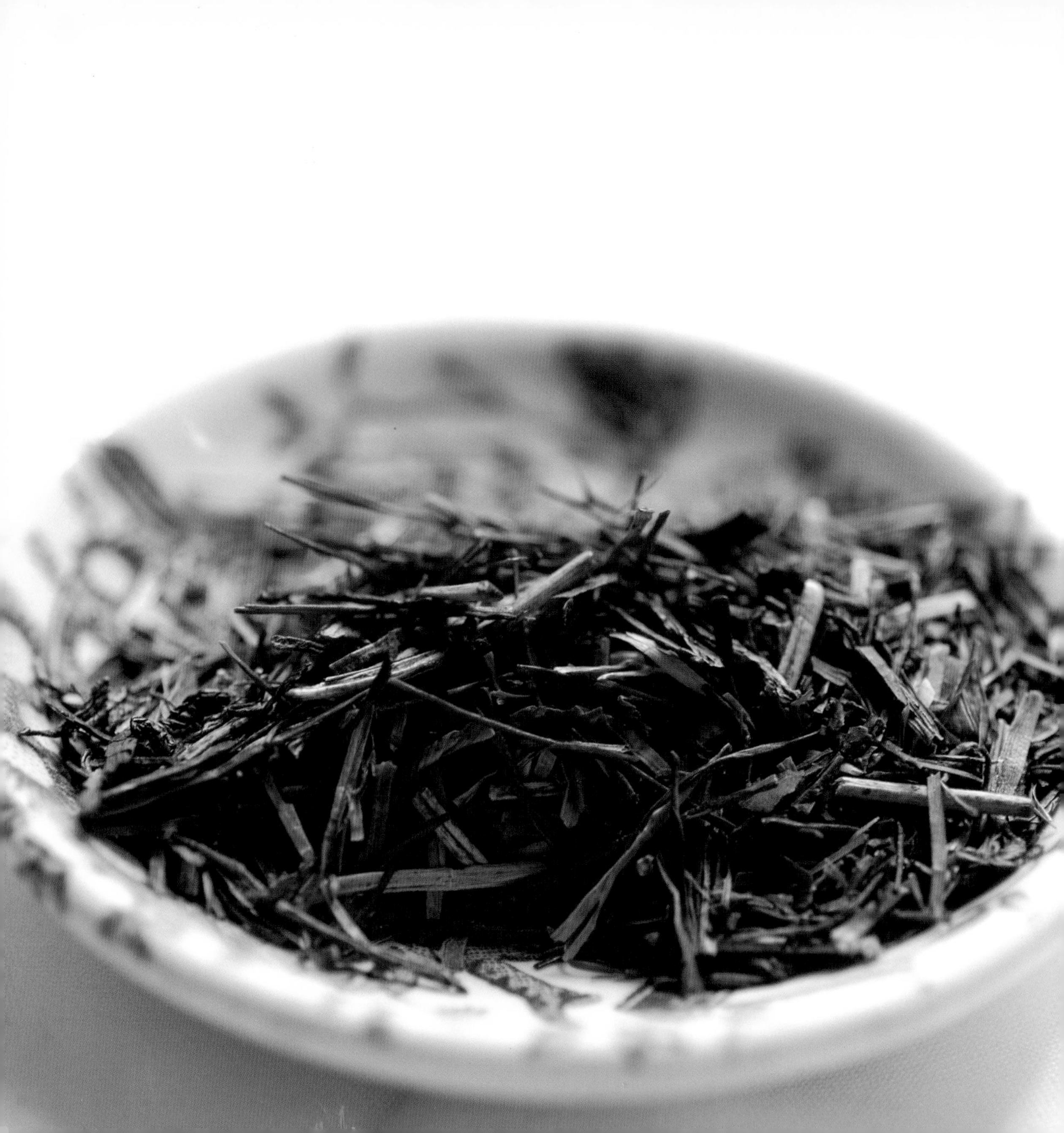

STEEPED

IN THE WORLD OF TEA

EDITED BY SHARON BARD, BIRGIT NIELSEN, AND CLARA ROSEMARDA
PHOTOGRAPHY BY JULIANA SPEAR

Interlink Books

An imprint of Interlink Publishing Group, Inc.
Northampton, Massachusetts

First published in 2005 by

INTERLINK BOOKS

An imprint of Interlink Publishing Group, Inc.
46 Crosby Street, Northampton, Massachusetts 01060
www.interlinkbooks.com

Library of Congress Cataloging-in-Publication Data
Steeped in the world of tea / edited by Sharon Bard, Birgit Nielsen, and
Clara Rosemarda ; photography by Juliana Spear.—1st American ed.
p. cm.
ISBN 1-56656-556-1 (pbk.)
1. Tea. 2. Cookery (Tea) 3. Tea—Anecdotes. I. Bard, Sharon. II. Nielsen, Birgit.
III. Rosemarda, Clara.
TX817.T3S73 2004
341.3'372—dc22

2004011289

Acknowledgments
We thank Oz Shelach, Charlotte Richardson, Mary Jean Haley and Bob Rice for their support of
this project. We would like to give special thanks to Wendy Rouder for all her work and sage
advice that helped bring this book to publication. Thanks to the late Donna Merritt Smith for
bringing us together at her Thursday writing group.

Credits
Stephen Levine's "Making a Cup of Green Tea, I Stop the War" was adapted with his
permission from his book, *Healing Into Life and Death*, Anchor Books Doubleday,
New York: 1989. (Thanks to Susan Barber for arranging permission.)
Tolbert McCarroll's "Tea Cups and Christmas Angels" was first published in
The Press Democrat, December 24, 2000 © Tolbert McCarroll

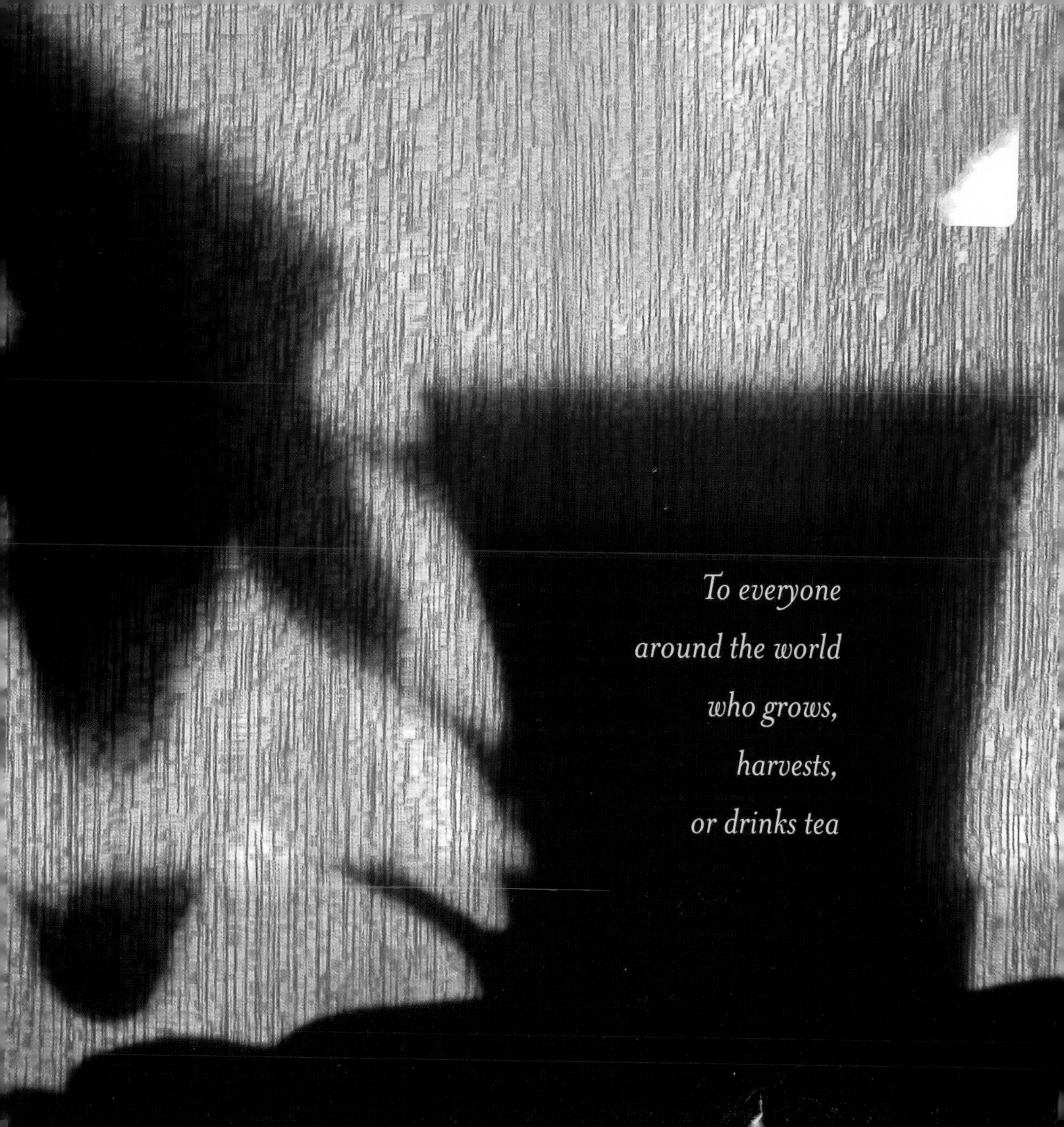

To everyone
around the world
who grows,
harvests,
or drinks tea

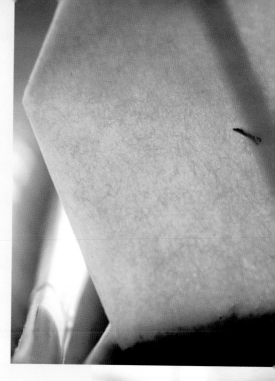

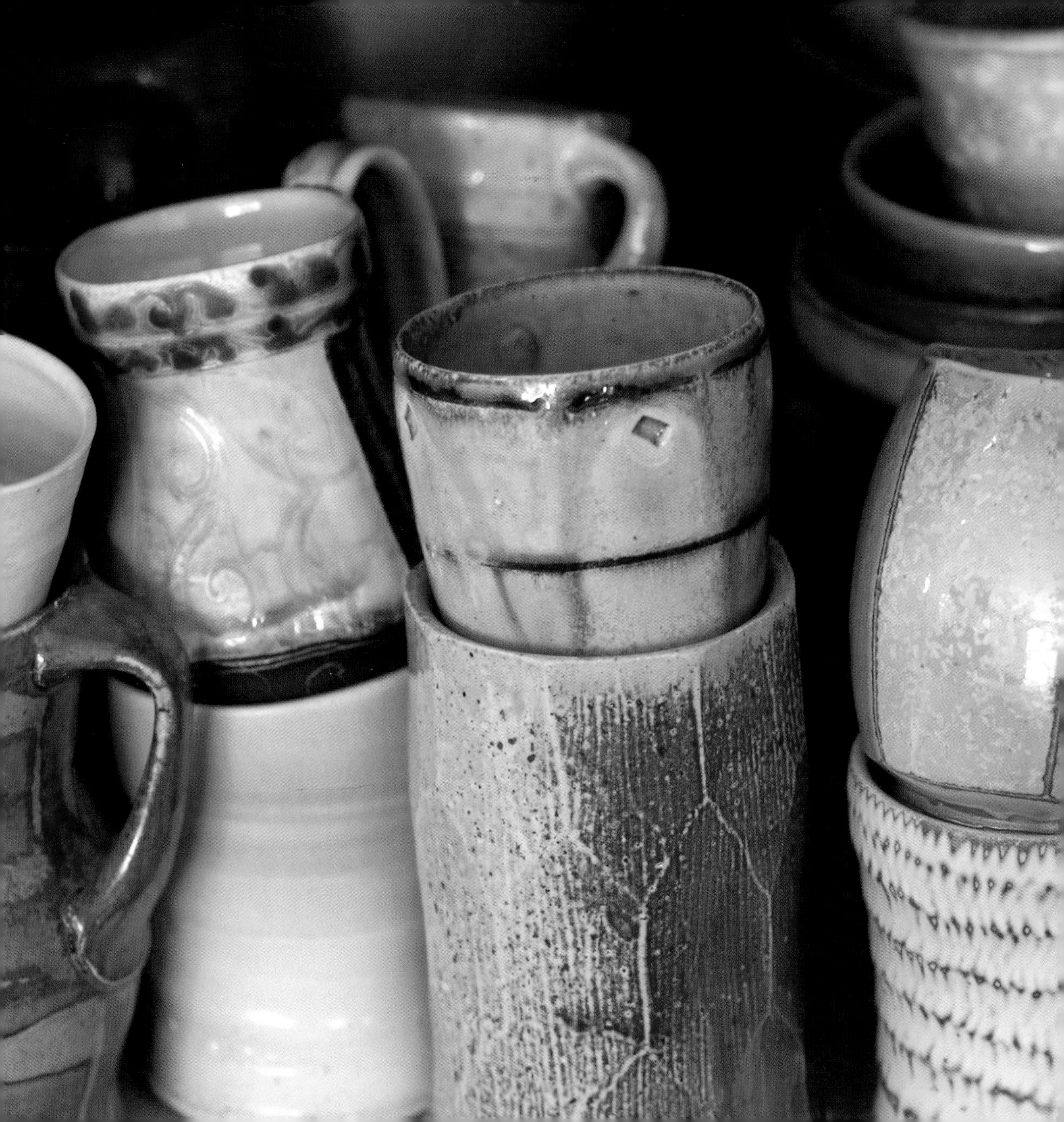

Introduction

This book emerged from a conversation over after-dinner tea in Northern California. Several of the editors had eaten Thai green curry and were drinking green tea from bone china cups. As we emptied our cups, the face of a young Asian woman smiled at us from the bottom of the cup. We, too, smiled and began to tell stories. It started with the story of the tea set: where did these gaudy, red and gold-trimmed cups and teapot with a bamboo handle come from?

Our inherited and adopted backgrounds couldn't have been more different: we were Japanese, Russian-Jewish, German, and American, from the wild West and the genteel South. As the hours passed and our stories brewed and poured forth, we realized that we had much in common. We each had rich, beautiful stories about tea. What additional stories might we hear if we asked others to join in and tell their tales?

Tea is ritual and ceremony that has been passed on in old and new ways for 5,000 years. People drink tea in nearly every country, and tea is second only to water in worldwide consumption. Tea has survived conflicts between empires and nations. It will survive us.

The stories in this collection span the globe from Russia to Japan, Kenya to Palestine, China to Latin America, Germany to Sumatra. Whether you are sipping tea from a bone china cup, a glass, or an unadorned earthenware vessel, we encourage you to take your time, enjoy and steep yourself in these stories.

Lastly, a special thank you to our contributors for their continued patience, support, and for sharing our vision. Without you, this book would not be here.

Be well and drink tea,
—the Editors

Monkey-Picked Oolong

by Marc E. Hofstadter

Meditating on this yellow liquor
pale and shimmering in a porcelain cup,
I become liquid myself,
poised on nothingness,
a quiet monk in a forgotten valley.

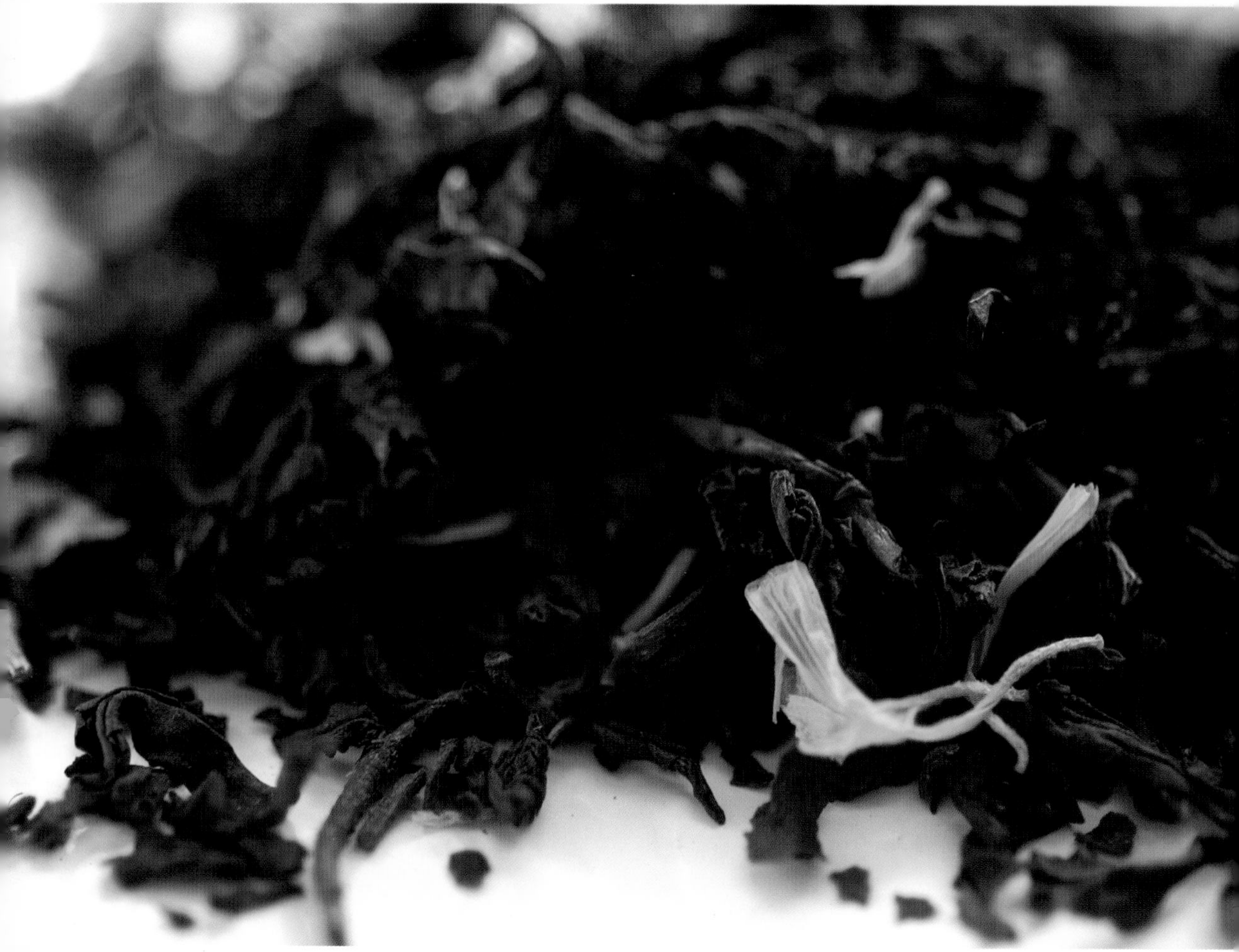

DR. FU'S TEA

by Lorraine Ash

I am a long way from the Lipton's and lemon of my childhood sick days when I open a clear plastic bag from Dr. Fu. I untie his Chinese pharmacist's knot and the leaves, roots, seeds, berries, and bark cascade into my roaster pan. Dry and brittle, they tinkle against the side.

They smell like tobacco, licorice and flowers, like Dr. Fu's office on the eighth floor of a Chinatown office building.

The directions for my fertility tea are so simple, they calm me: Add 24 cups of water to contents; boil for two hours; keep refrigerated; drink three times a day, after meals.

I fill the roaster with water and set the flame under the pan, imagining a Chinese woman in a land far away, 2,000 years ago, drinking such a tea.

Steam rises over my pan, like mist over the Yunnan Mountains. I see it against the night sky outside my window, and I wonder why I believe in these ancient blends more than I do in the injections and insertions and drugs of my own civilization.

Maybe it was the way the woman at the reproductive medicine institute answered when I called and asked how effective Chinese herbal teas are for infertility. There was a pause.

"Is this a joke?" she asked.

"No."

"Chinese tea?"

"Yes," I said.

"Ask me about Clomid."

"What about Clomid?"

"I'll send you an information sheet."

I believe in Dr. Fu, I think, because he doesn't have information sheets. I like his white hair and warm eyes and that the window next to his desk and index card filing system is dirty with smog, the sill lined with thank you cards and pictures of his patients' children in pretty clothes.

"Twins!" he said when my husband and I first went to see him. He held out a picture of two girls and smiled.

Maybe I believe in the tea because Dr. Fu charges $45 for a month's work—$4 for the herbs, $41 for the mixing—and because the fertility doctor's business is Clomid, then something stronger, then

artificial insemination, then in vitro fertilization for $25,000.

Maybe I believe in my tea because of Dr. Fu's confidence—"Don't worry, OK?"—or because he never insists, as many people do, that things will work out because that's the fair thing to happen in life. I already know that isn't true. My daughter, my first and only child, was stillborn at full term, lost on the last day of a perfect pregnancy to an infection that started inside me, betraying both of us for no reason.

Maybe I believe in the tea because I lost faith in the invincibility of God and because Dr. Fu comes from a

15

land of Buddha, another god.

Maybe I believe because when my daughter died I lost faith in science. My daughter had passed every prenatal test devised until, at the last moment, her heart stopped. Maybe I like the tea because China is filled with infant and toddler girls waiting to be daughters and it's imposible for me not to respond to that.

Maybe it's because this tea is medicine from the Earth and the Earth knows in ways people can't.

Maybe it's because the tea knows me better than I know myself. It knows what to do, I think. And if something can be done, it will do it. And if nothing can be done, it will not insist there's something wrong with it or me or Buddha or the Earth.

I don't know why I drink this tea and behold these leaves and roots, seeds, berries, and bark like a person who isn't yet but will be a friend when the right circumstance allows the two of us to open and fill each other.

Maybe drinking this tea is drinking hope, gently. There's no sugar in real hope, and I like that my tea tastes like murky water. Hope shouldn't taste good.

This old tea is a companion as I float from an ocean of sadness into one of possibility. I don't know why I trust it, but I do. If I knew, if I liked its taste, if I understood it, if it promised me something, if it spoke to me in words, it would lose its magic.

I close my eyes when I drink it, wherever I am, because sometimes I've poured it in a thermos and have taken it with me. When I drink it I picture that woman in China in a rice paddy, millennia ago. And I drink. And I dream and I drink.

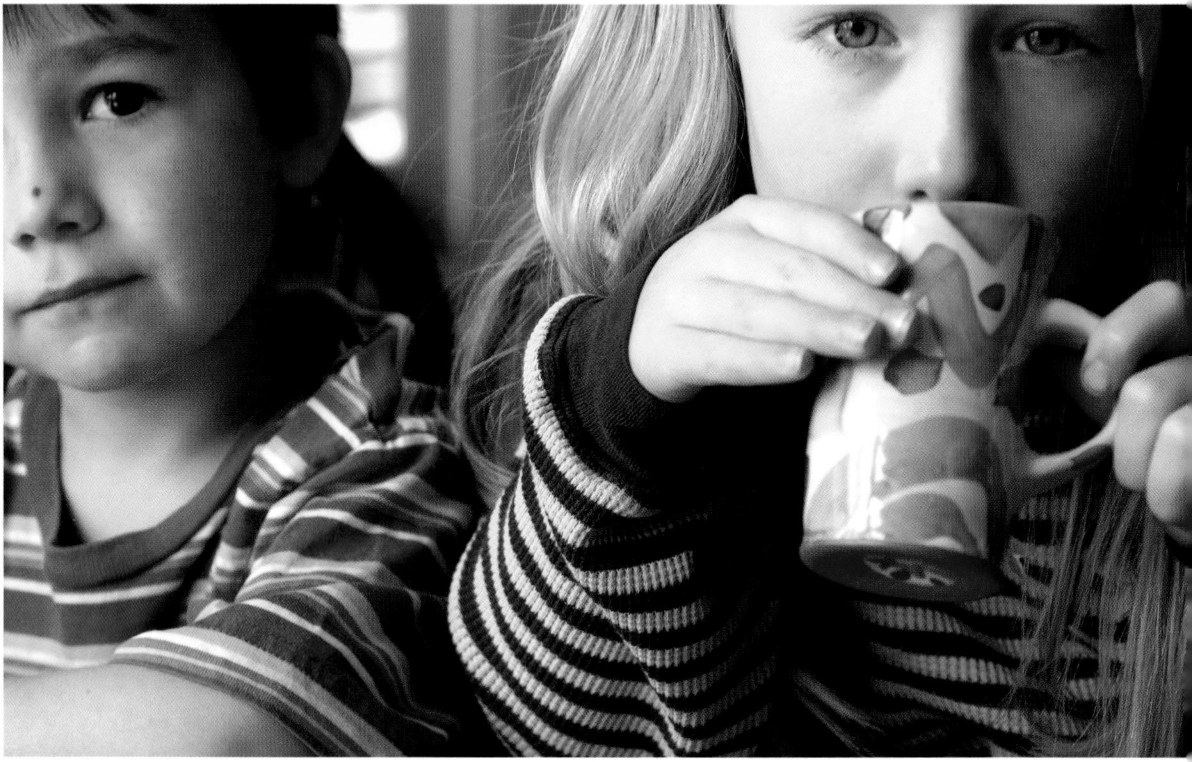

A Geography of Tea

by Noreen Quinn-Singh

Come in and have a cup of tea was probably the sentence I heard most growing up in Ireland. A kettle of water was always on the range in case someone called. We drank tea for breakfast, in the early afternoon, for supper, and for the many breaks in between. Nothing was considered worse than weak—pronounced *wake*—tea without milk and sugar. It was very sad to hear of a new wife in the community, "Ah, sure, she doesn't even know how to make a cup of tea!"

The ultimate insult was to offer tea without something to eat with it—a slice of bread with jam, some biscuits or, if one was lucky, a piece of homemade apple or rhubarb pie. Each season had its favorite tea accompaniment. In autumn it was the traditional barn brack, with a ring inside over which we children fought. For three weeks in December, it was Christmas cake. This was the Queen of cakes, with icing to suit the occasion. Almond only was for frequent callers, while cake with both almond and white icing was for special,

less frequent visitors. In spring, when there were plenty of eggs and butter, Mama made scones. We sliced them in the middle and slathered country butter on top. The big family teapot was filled at least twice whenever we had scones.

The vocabulary used in tea-making varied from that of our neighbors in England. They brewed their tea; we drew it. They put on the kettle but we put it down, maybe a leftover from the time when the people had to bend down to hang the big kettle over the coals. The English "Would you like a cup of tea?" was considered too formal and hesitant in Ireland.

The idea was to make callers think it would be very hurtful to say no, so they were given very little space to say no in. "You'll have a cup of tea while you're waiting," or "I'll add your name to the pot." Even a no was, and to some extent remains, "No, but ask me again." Now I live in France, where yes is affirmative and no a closed subject, but when I visit my neighbors in Ireland, and they delight in my Irish accent after all the years away, "Ah, sure, you haven't changed a bit," how can I possibly refuse their hospitality?

There were two ways to start and bond a friendship in Ireland: having a drink together in a pub and having a cup of tea at someone's home. The woman of the house poured and we sat, talked and listened. As in a confessional, tea loosened the tongue and set the stage for sharing. "Did you hear about poor so and so and…?" My mother never gossiped or told what she called "bad luck stories," so it was over tea at a neighbor's that at last I learned what was common knowledge. As I sipped, suddenly things became clearer—the sudden departures, the silences, and even, God forbid, the guards' car outside somebody's house. The mystery unfolded as I drank my way to a second teapot. I might have thought I would not be able to finish a whole banana sandwich, but in the excitement of the details, I went through a piece of apple pie and cream and a queen cake and then was on my second biscuit.

Despite a full bladder, I didn't dare stop the lady in her stride with the teapot, lest she withhold any tiny detail. I was grateful to this person for all the entertainment, and I searched for a story to swap. If I didn't have one, I fell back on a recent joke or a riddle I'd heard. The ideal was to keep the clincher until the end as I put down my empty cup. If I could somehow make the joke connect with what I'd heard; a sort of moral-of-the-story-is… then I had it made. "Ah, Noreen is great craic all right, you know what she said as she was leaving…." For "craic" was prized in the community I came from. What good were all your degrees, experience, and sophistication if you couldn't make others laugh with you? You had to claim all as your own, though. No laws against plagiarism there, where Josie down the road was equal to Yeats, Frost, or Shakespeare. I stored what I heard in long-term memory, to be used to suit my own tea occasions.

Tea was bought in bulk. It came in big tea chests, and the shopkeepers packaged it themselves. Our local shopkeepers used to give us the empty ones, a useful commodity on the farm. When newborn lambs were sick, we administered a few drops of poteen and

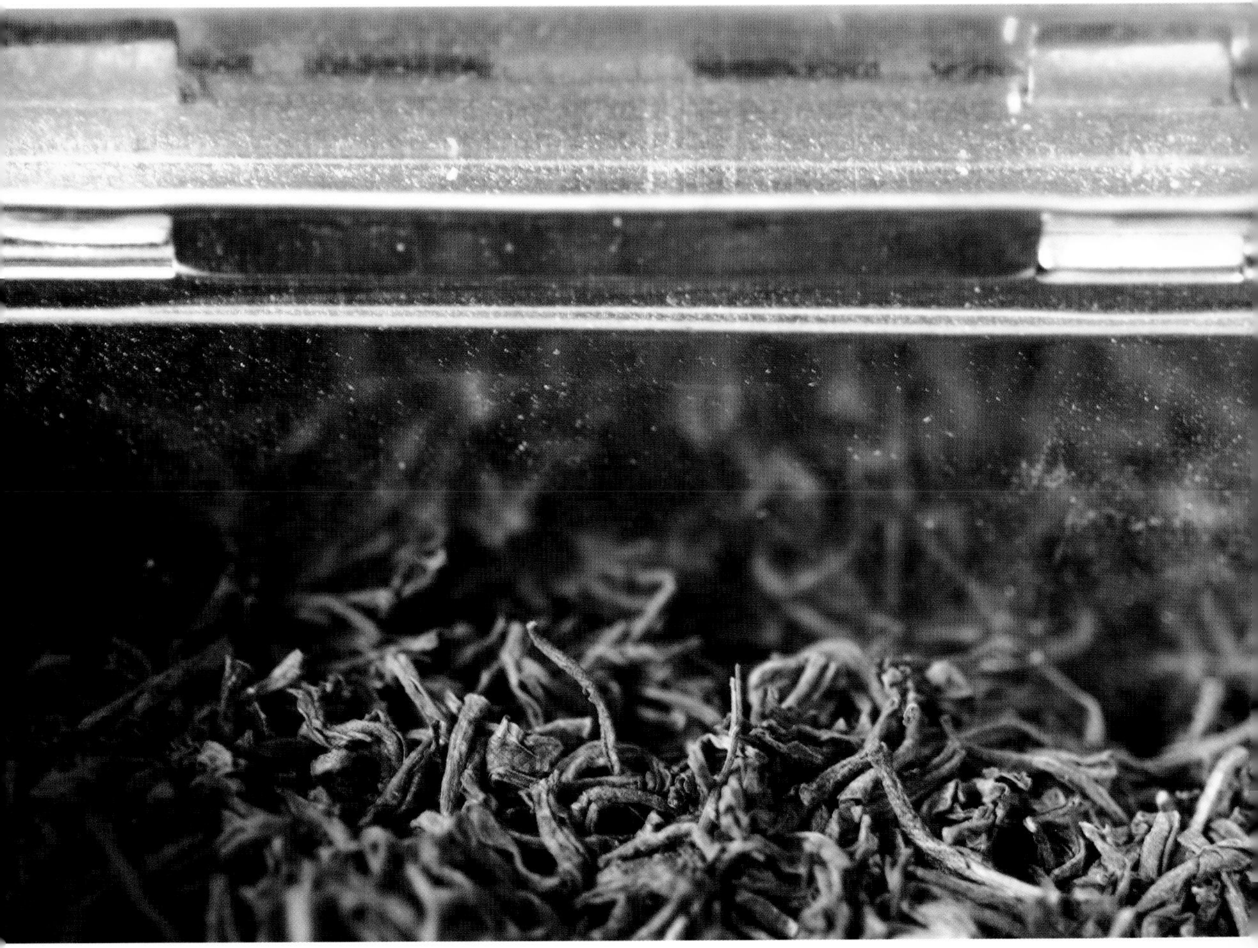

left them near the range in the kitchen, in the tea-container. There, they lived for a day or two, while we children stroked and played with them, knowing that it would not be possible to approach them once they were out in nature. Some of our neighbors used the chests to store their provisions of flour for making bread. On my travels in India and Africa, I have seen the same type of tea chest turned on its side and used as table, or seat.

We children grew up on tea, very milky at first, so that we would not burn our tongues. Our school was too far away to come home for lunch, so we brought our lunches of brown bread and jam, with tea in winter and milk in summer. The master heated up the tea near the open fire, placing all the bottles around in rows. Sometimes the corks popped off when the bottles became too hot. The aroma of tea mingled with the smell of wet coats and the timber in the sawmill out back and planted the seed of my desire to travel. When I went outside to the toilet I looked at the timber and dreamed of Canada and Australia. I knew even then that tea in my house and small school was just the starting point on my journey.

In most of the countries I have lived , tea found me. In Cameroon we didn't live in the high grasslands where the cows were pastured, so we had to settle for imported tinned milk with tea or drink it black. We learned to like both. By the time I got to France, I was ready for the biologicals and infusions—herbals for the real tea connoisseur. After a fine meal, my friends offer me a *tisane*, an infusion, to be sipped slowly from a precious-looking teacup and saucer, invariably an heirloom.

Perhaps one reason I was so much at home in India from the beginning was that the country rivals Ireland in tea-drinking. Chai is a legacy of the British. Water, tea, sugar, and milk are boiled together to produce a concoction that took a little getting used to. It is best when green cardamom is

added. I first tried chai on a second-class train. A man with a huge kettle and a bucket of china cups walked the whole length of the train, pouring here and there, collecting the money at the same time, retrieving the cups on his return trip. Now, paper or plastic has replaced the crockery, and chai has become tea. As with tea in Ireland and England, chai is accompanied by cake, biscuits, or *burfi*, a rich sweet made with milk and eaten at Diwali, the festival of lights, in October or November. The luxurious ones have almonds and other goodies in them.

I was also introduced to the custom of "bed tea" in India, and we continue to have it in France, especially on the weekends. Strong, it's drunk in bed on an empty stomach to wake you up and get you going. I go for Barry's Irish tea then, and we call it bed tea even if we drink it walking around our living room. It's my link with India, first thing in the morning. I can almost hear the traffic with the horns going, can see the crowds already up and moving.

In Ireland we never measured tea. It was spooned from the packet into the warmed teapot, and sometimes someone would read the leaves to tell the future. In my husband's household, Mamaji scoops out the tea the same way my mother used to. Her natural inclination is to pour chai straight from the teapot, but for me she strains it first. I wonder if I should tell her that it is nice for me to see all the tea leaves, at a time when tea bags have taken over in Ireland, and in France all kinds of gadgets contain the leaves. I marvel that though I have married into a family at the other end of the world whose customs, religion, and way of life are so different, tea binds us together.

Tea helps us celebrate the joys and lessen the misfortunes we meet in life. The world at our feet, our secondary school and university successes were rejoiced over in a café. When my husband stopped wearing his turban and had his long hair cut for the first time, he helped me get over the grief by making tea. Most of all, I remember the three months when my mother lay at home battling cancer. We made tea for all the neighbors and friends who came to see her. Death may have been approaching the bedroom, but as long as our family had a kitchen full of friends, life, and tea, we were ready.

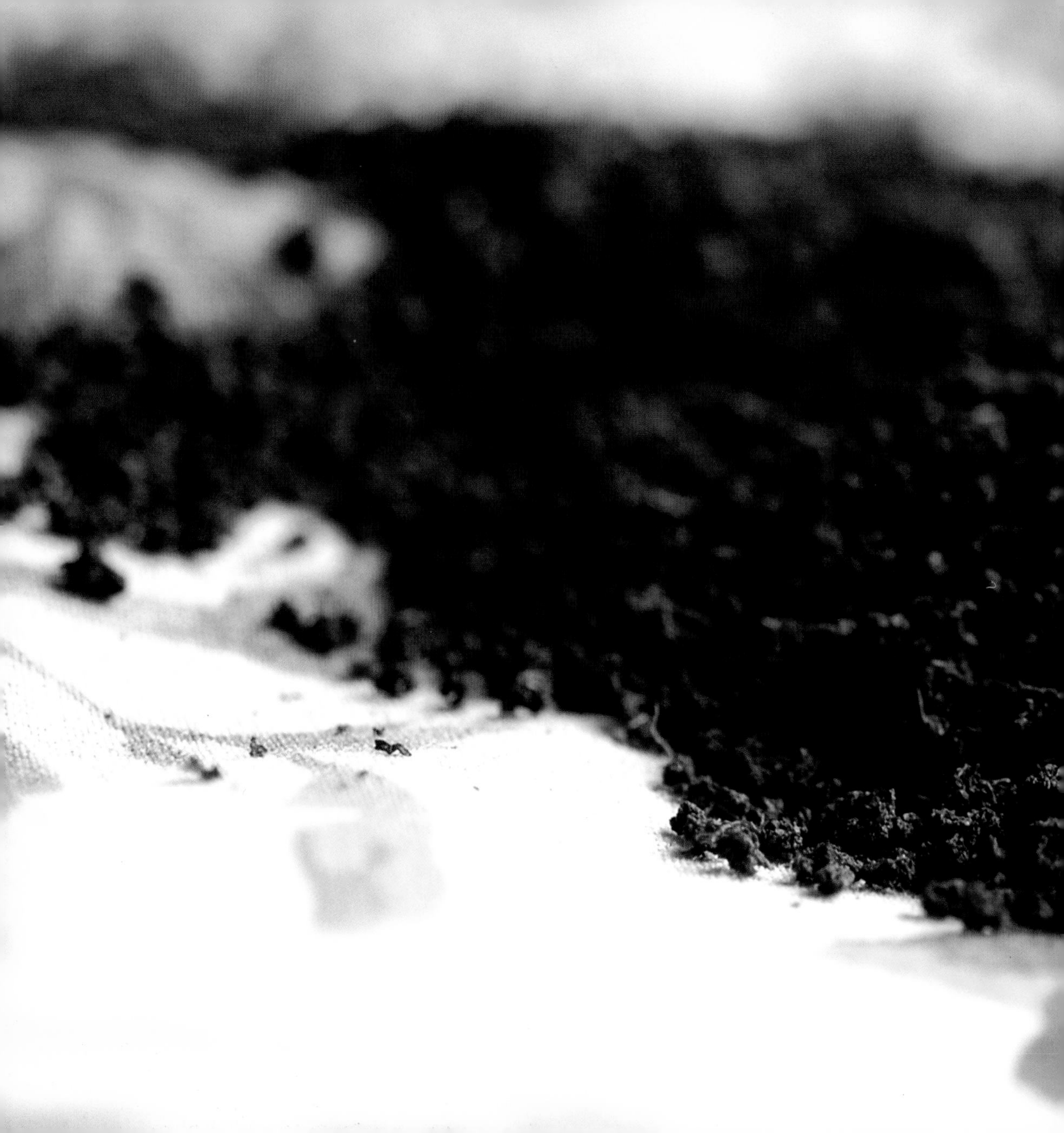

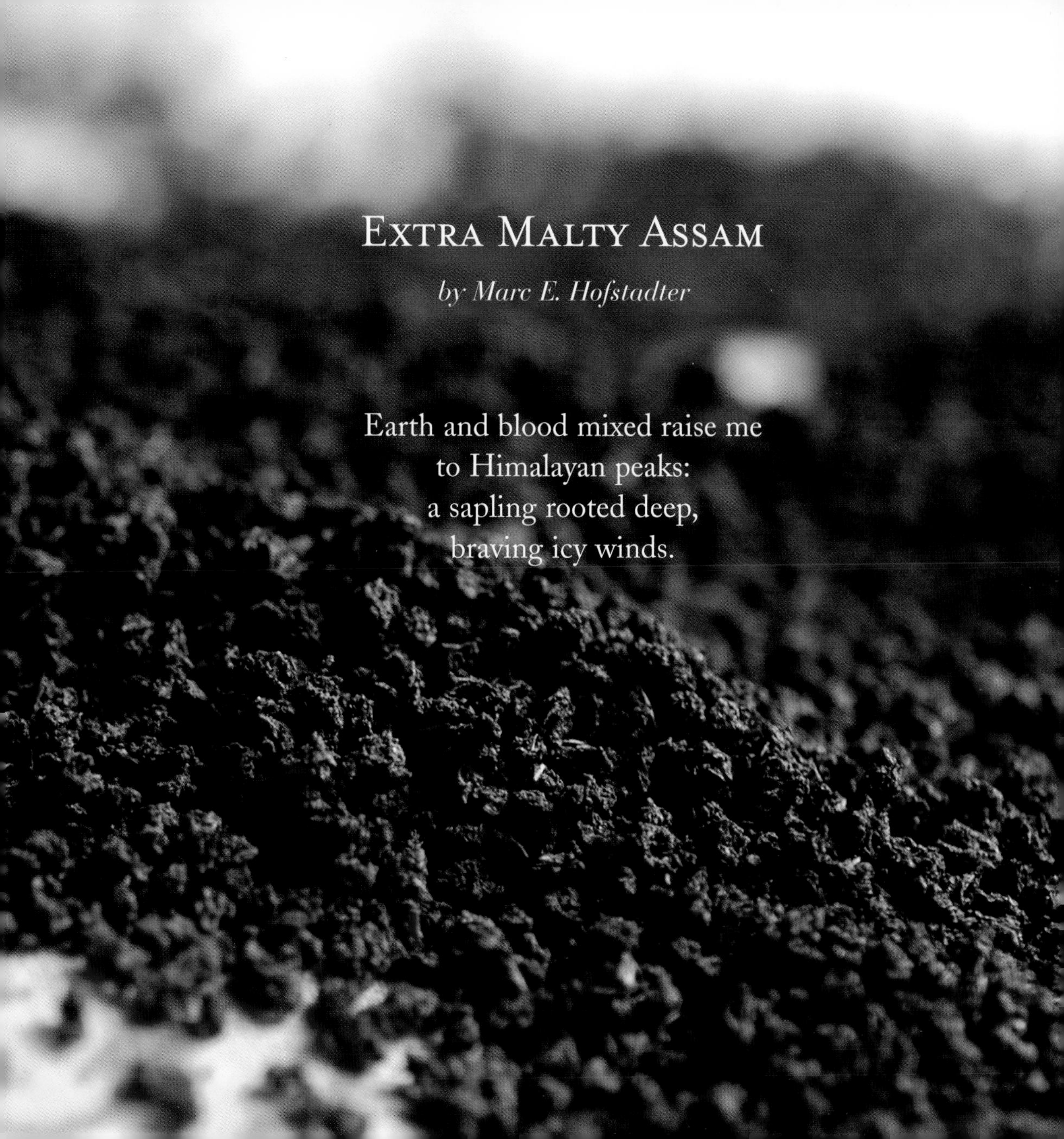

Extra Malty Assam

by Marc E. Hofstadter

Earth and blood mixed raise me
to Himalayan peaks:
a sapling rooted deep,
braving icy winds.

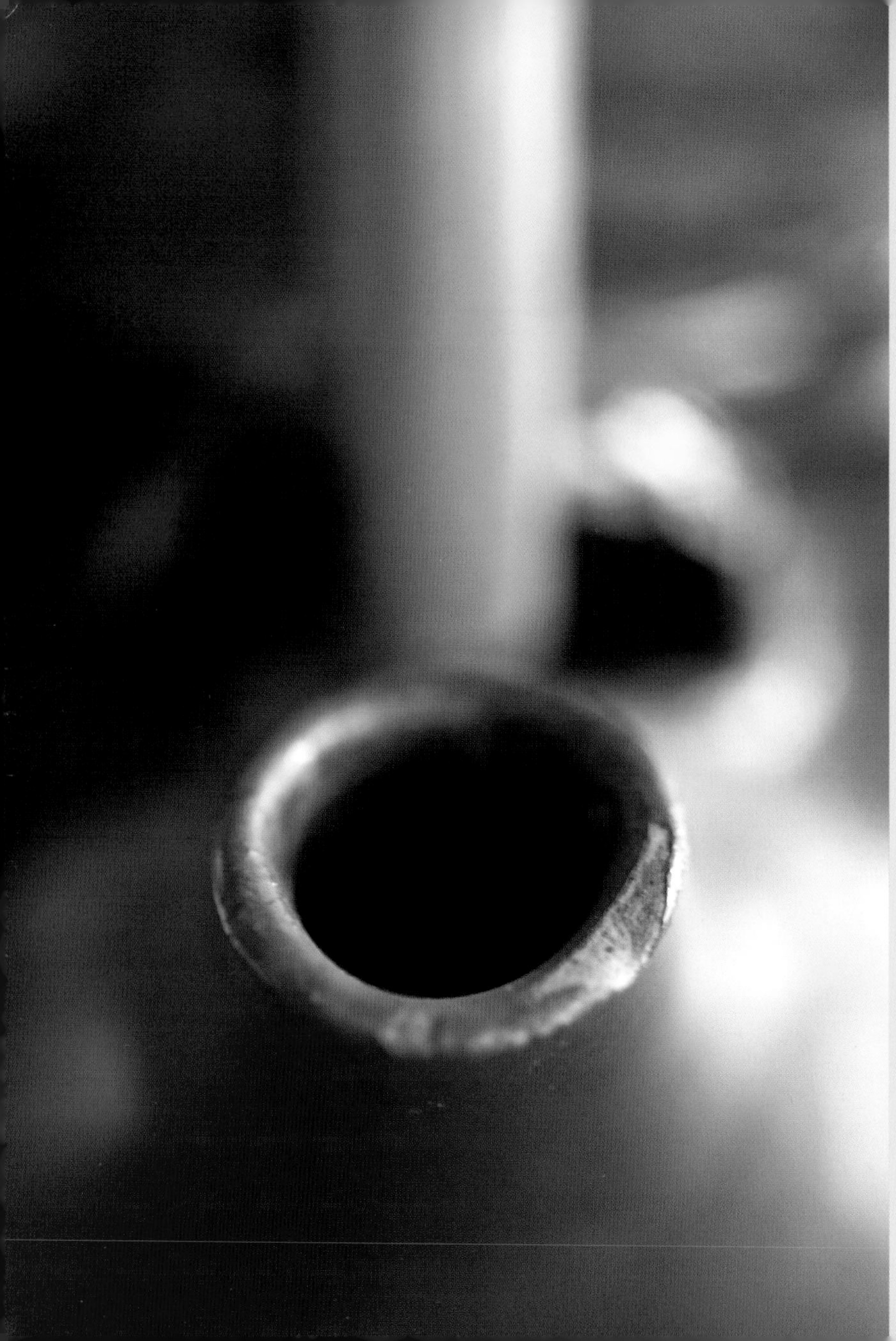

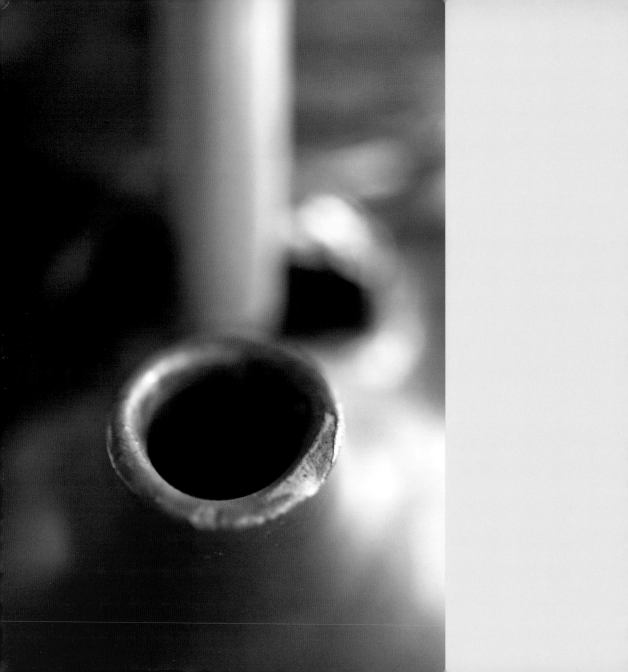

PICNIC TEA ON FLAG HILL

by Marguerite Thoburn Watkins

This afternoon we decide to climb Flag Hill to see if, after fifty years, it is still strung with prayer flags. I am part of a group who grew up in the Himalayas, and we are revisiting Mussoorie, sixty miles from the Tibetan border. We will be gone at teatime so our hosts pack a picnic tea. A leisurely afternoon tea has been a tradition here since the British founded this pleasant Indian hill station. We climb single-file straight uphill on a narrow path through rhododendrons, ferns, silver oaks, and October asters. On the first low crest flutter a few Tibetan prayer flags of bleached white muslin, the writing completely gone.

We pass a succession of small clearings. Each has been a campsite, for there is a circle of blackened stones in the center. We toil upwards for a mile, panting for breath at this elevation and because we are carrying the huge metal canister of hot tea. A Tibetan woman and her helper carry the food.

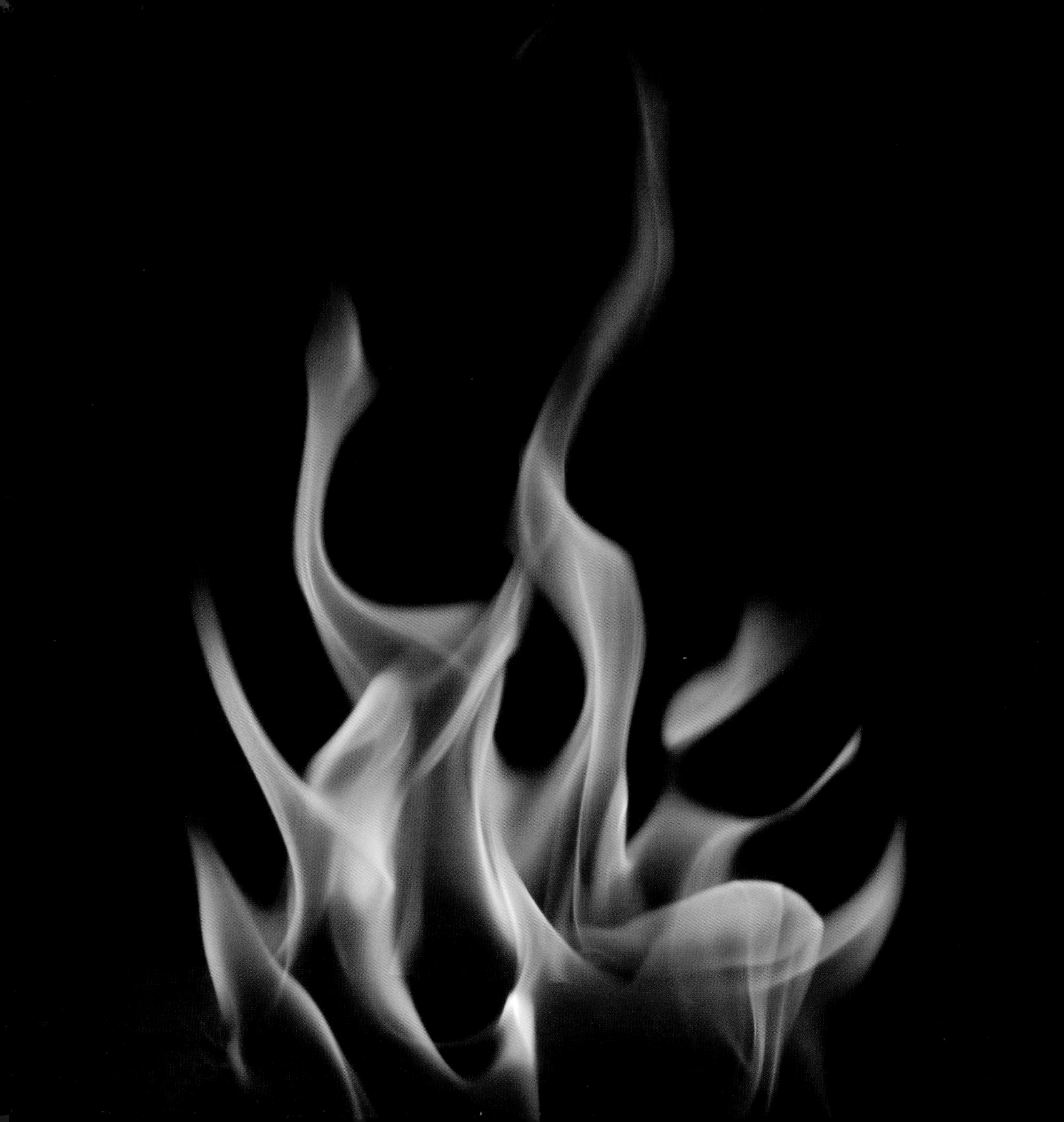

And now we are at the summit, Flag Hill, no disappointment. To the sides of this high bald are wind-stunted silver oaks, one fairly large one serving as the center of an irregular wheel of weathered rope-strung Buddhist prayer flags. Hundreds of white or faded crimson squares flap in a stiff breeze. In the middle of the clearing is a large fire circle filled with charred wood pieces and half-burned flags.

"When a flag falls to the ground it is thrown in the fire," says Tensing, a Tibetan friend. "Fire is sacred. But it is all right if you want to take one."

I smooth out a partially burned piece of cloth. Tibetan script frames an outline of a leaping horse, the favorite mount of a famous king.

"He actually lived," says Tensing.

Far below us are hills—bare, terraced, or forested where protected from the wind. They are green, for the rainy season has just ended. Mist rolls in, obscuring the southern view. Northward the sun gilds range upon range. Distant clouds hide distant snows.

The Tibetan woman serves savory fried snacks on leaf plates. We have a hot sauce for dipping and eat with our fingers. Our tea is a satisfying scalding Indian chai; the milk, sugar, and water have been

33

boiled with the tea leaves, then left to simmer into this robust brew. It is drink and food fit for the gods—nectar and ambrosia. I blow on my tea before I sip it. It tastes of cardamon, ginger, clove, and black pepper.

Above my head, prayer flags flap in the wind, some weathered soft and thin, some retaining colors and scriptures. Mist, the wispy remnant of the just-ended monsoon, swirls in, swirls out; now concealing, now revealing valleys and ranges. As it parts, the hillsides shine in a wash of late afternoon sunlight. I dangle my feet over the sheer drop below me; I would be afraid to look down were it not for the white curtain of protection. Surely I am in heaven, or as close as I am likely to get in this lifetime—an American traveler on a Himalayan mountain at British teatime sipping Indian chai under Tibetan prayer flags.

Finally we burn the leaf plates, and I throw a fallen flag into the flames, grateful that the tea has given me a reason to linger here an hour.

Tibetans live on the other side of Mussoorie now, refugees from Chinese persecution, but there have always been prayer flags here, strung by transient traders traveling from their high plateau behind the mountains. I remember seeing the traders as I walked home from school; they were herding lines of long-haired goats, each carrying two small saddle-bags of salt. These flags, so far from any habitation, still mark the devotion of Himalayan travelers on their way between Tibet and India. They string them above their campsites, leaving their prayers on the highest points, the most remote, where thousands of times an hour the winds can send them toward heaven.

And I am glad that the campsite fire circles have been recently used and that as night falls the traders are still cooking lentils and warming their hands over the fire until they can cup them around their own glasses of hot tea. They add salt and butter to their chai; it comforts the belly after the hard day, and warms the hands and heart.

MAKING TEA

by Judith Grey

Polish a pot.
Follow a path to a well
by an empty cottage
waiting like an unwound watch.
Stand on a hollow well head
above a ring of rock.
Fill a dented pail
left there for passing thirst.
Spill some
just to hear it disappear
with hollow dripping back into the source.
Pour a waterfall into a pot.
Fling the remains on a tangled garden.
Return stepping clear of grasshoppers
clicking a warning or a love song.

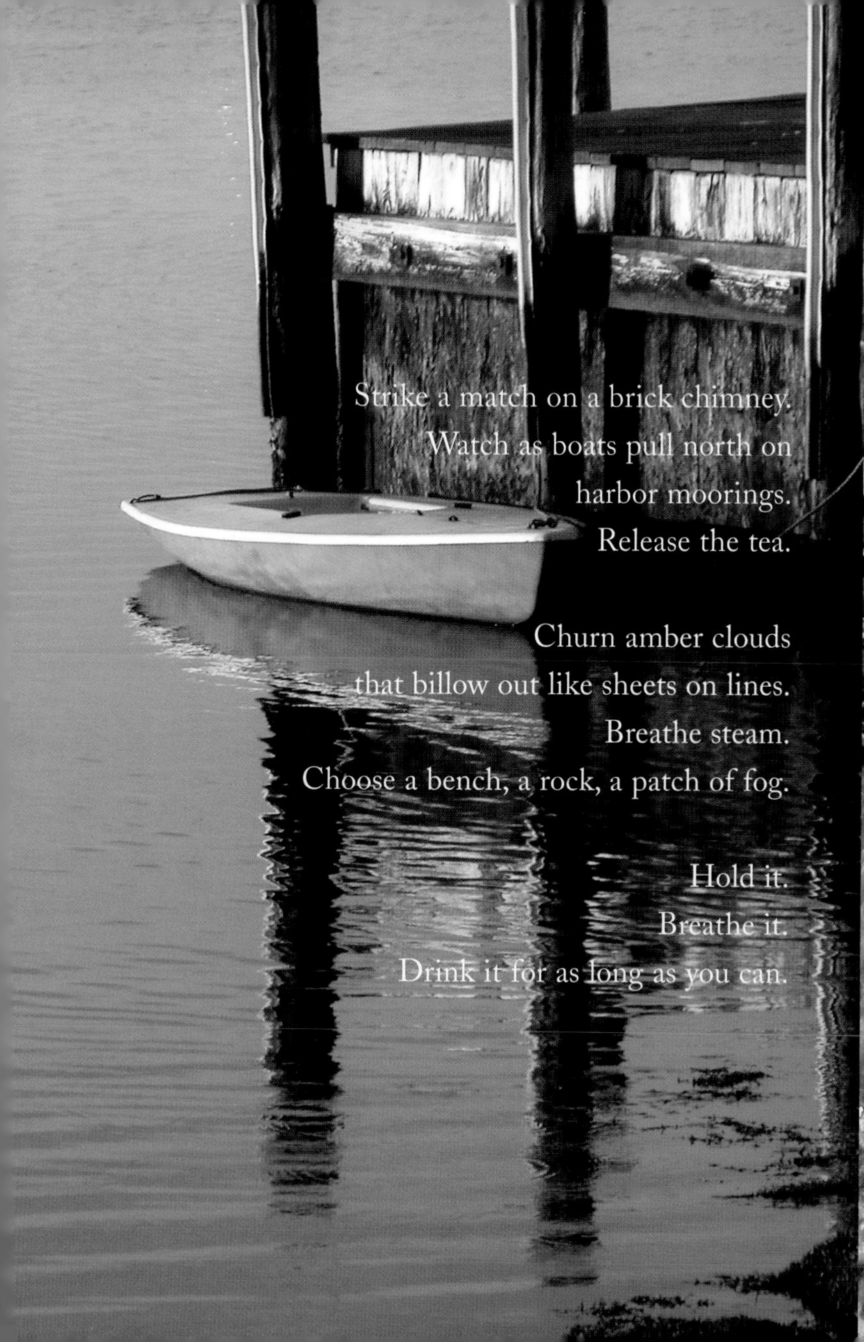

Strike a match on a brick chimney.
Watch as boats pull north on
harbor moorings.
Release the tea.

Churn amber clouds
that billow out like sheets on lines.
Breathe steam.
Choose a bench, a rock, a patch of fog.

Hold it.
Breathe it.
Drink it for as long as you can.

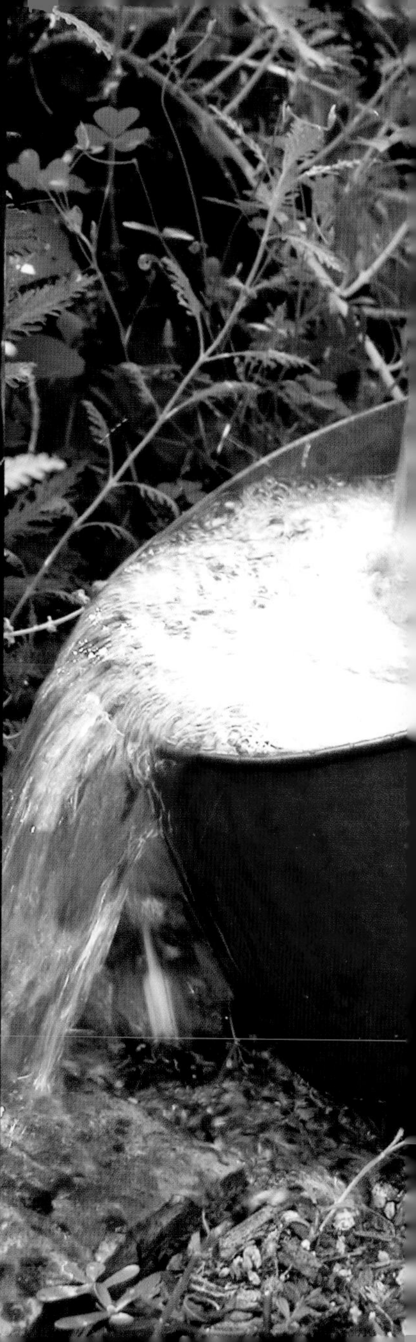

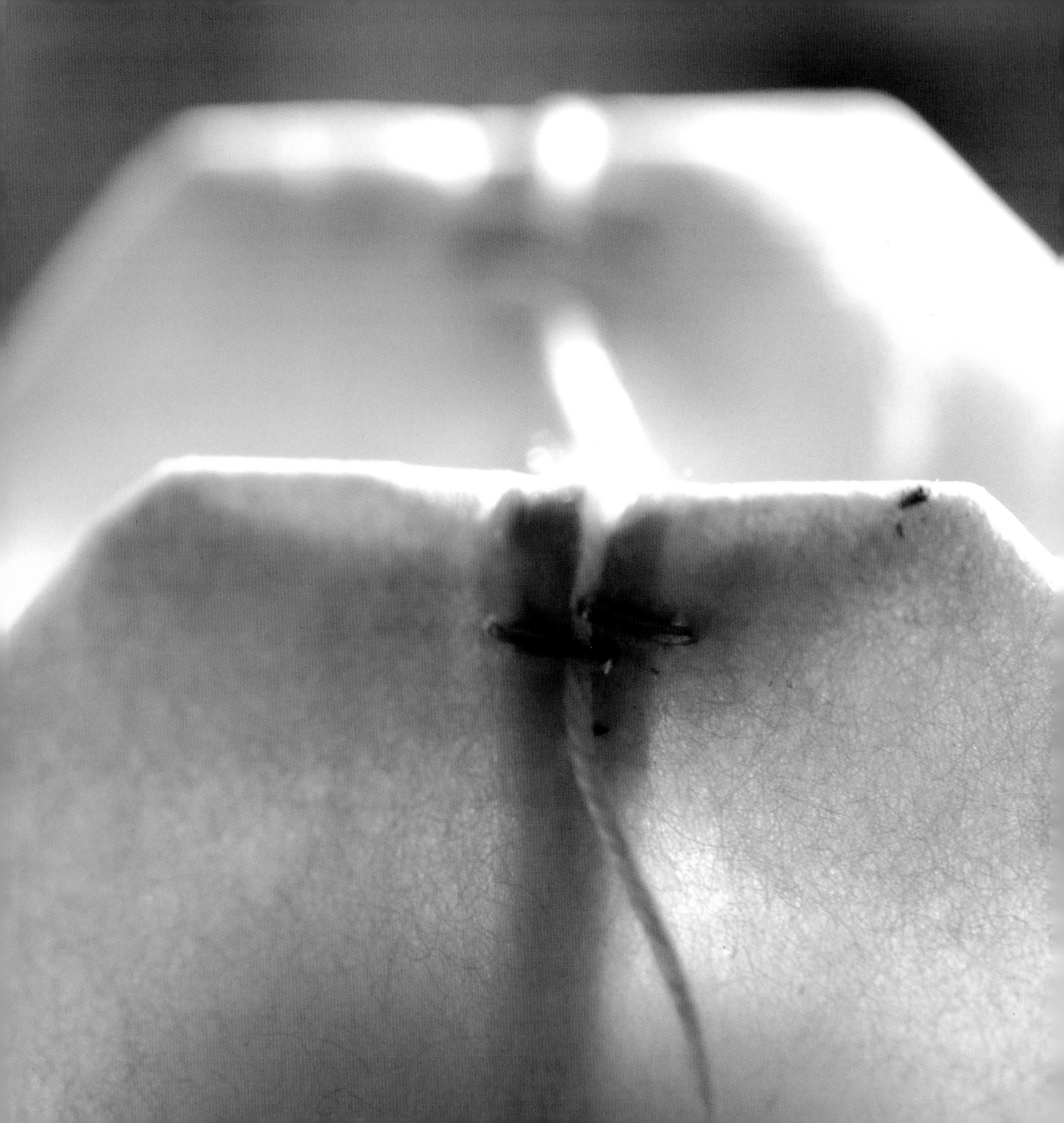

THE WINE OF THE POOR

by Arthur Dobrin

Which to believe—
The eyelids of a holy man
falling to earth and sprouting,
or a leaf silently descending
into an emperor's cup?
I consider this question
sipping
one day
Spring Jade,
another
Precious Dew.
I pour the queen of camellias,
look out my west window
at the rustling bamboo,
breathe in steam from a blue cup.
Drink slowly
this
exotic brew,
this
wine of the poor.

I discovered the pleasures of tea in 1963, the time I stumbled upon Empire coffee and tea importers on New York's 42nd Street, close by the Hudson River, where cruise ships and ocean liners docked. The store intrigued me. What is a tea importer? I wondered. I went in to find out and discovered that I could buy tea myself. Until then, I only knew Lipton's teabags, the kind my mother drank, never more than one cup a day, except when sick. She poured tepid water into a cup and dipped a tea bag once, twice, three times, then hung it on the side of a drinking glass and put it on the sink, to be used again and again. The bags lasted an entire week, turning stiffer and more brittle with every day. By the end of the week the water didn't change color at all and only she called it tea.

I learned to be frugal from my mother.

The day I walked into Empire coffee and tea importers, the wider world opened to me. Scattered throughout this dimly lit small warehouse were glass jars filled with loose tea. Some were behind the counter, some on the floor, there were scales to weigh the leaves, there were pamphlets describing the teas. As I looked around, I thought of the nearby ships ready to sail to distant ports hardly known to me at all: Assam and Darjeeling, Kandy and Sumatra. There was a reference

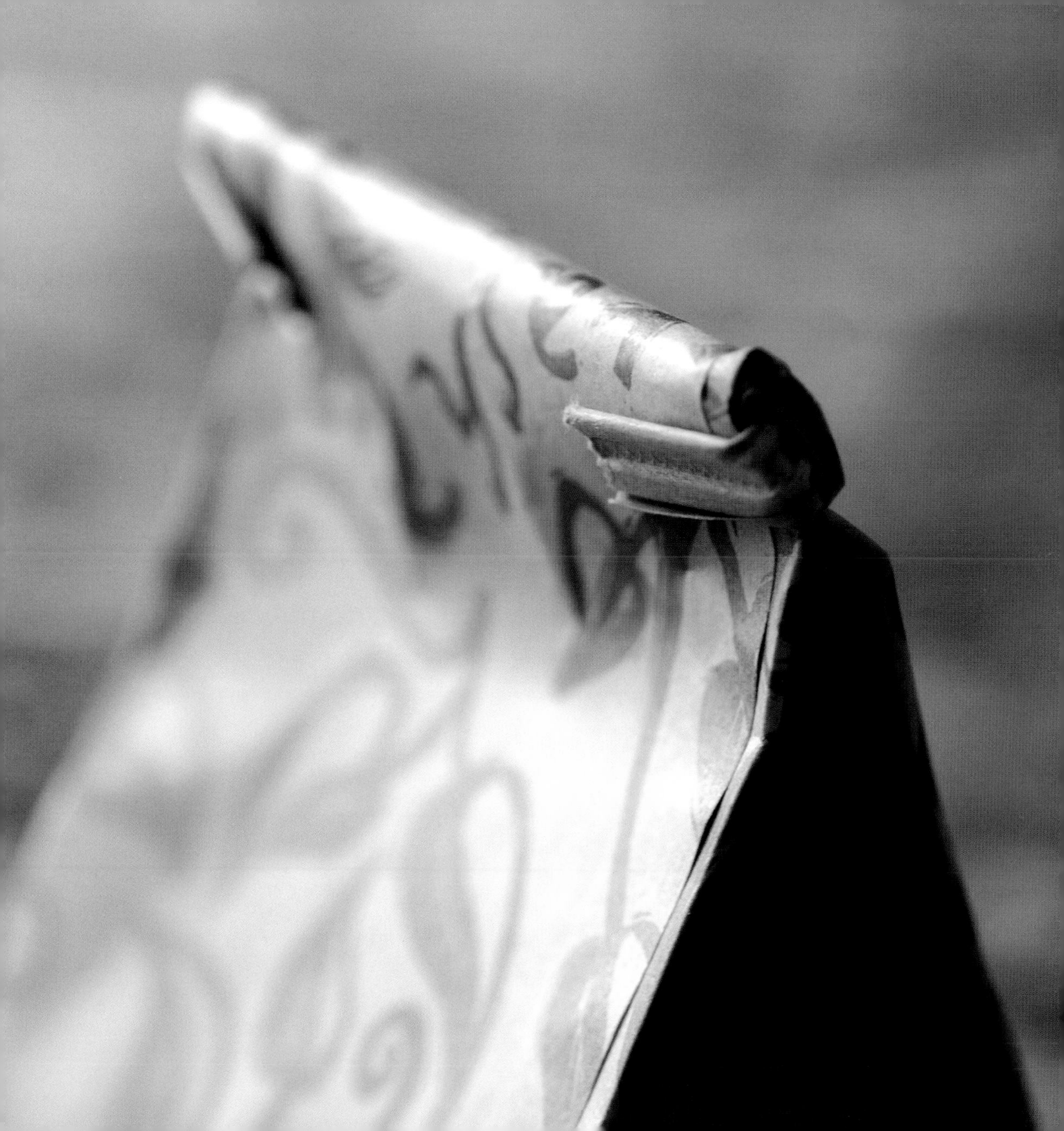

to a Russian caravan and breakfasts had by both the English and Irish. I didn't need the price of a transatlantic ticket to travel. Here for less than a dollar I could have blacks from India, oolongs and souchongs from China, greens from Japan. There were leaves scented with blossoms. I could drink something called Gunpowder. Such possibilities, such choices, such places. From then on, I bought a small amount every week to take home with me, to conjure faraway places at my kitchen table.

I bought books on tea and I learned the proper way to brew it—heat the tea pot, make sure the water is fresh, make sure it is boiling when poured, let it steep between three and five minutes. The drink turned out to be a thing far different than my mother's tinted water.

My romance with tea began at about the same time as my romance with Lyn. During our engagement she bought me an antique teapot with calligraphy incised on its side. After we were married, for about a week she even put a bowl on the fire escape of our Hackensack apartment to collect rainwater for me to use. I still have the pot she bought me, and it has a prominent place in our kitchen, where I admire it daily.

I began to search out new types and blends and whenever I found something I'd never tried before, I'd buy it. By the mid-1970s China began to export tea to America and now I couldn't keep up with the possibilities. I chose the tea by the attractiveness of the tins in which they were packaged. Some containers were round, some square, some were made of tin and some of bamboo. I bought tea because there was a picture of ancient scholars sitting on craggy rocks gazing into a snowy valley. Here were golden fish swimming in blue water, butterflies winging among jasmine flowers, a courtesan playing a lute. The containers were too beautiful to throw away, so I kept them. I don't have enough room to display them all, so many are packed in cartons in the attic. The most beautiful ones I keep out, on the shelves in the kitchen next to the refrigerator and on a shelf above my bedroom window.

Over the years I also have acquired many teapots. There's an unglazed blue one with a white dragon, several purple sand pots from Xixing, a Japanese cast-iron one, a large elegant glass pot for parties and two hand-carved soapstone teapots given to me by my friends in Kisii. Pots are dedicated for use with different teas and I use some only in particular seasons. The antique pot Lyn bought me has a hairline crack, so I use it sparingly.

Lyn and I once lived in western Kenya and continue to visit there often. One part of the country, from Kericho to Kisii, is so green and rolling that it looks like an emerald sea swelling as it recedes to the horizon. The odd thing is that it is impossible to drink a good cup of tea there. It isn't that the best tea is exported—the quality is consistently high wherever it is bought. Rather it is a problem with the high altitude, as we were about a mile above sea level. The water there simmers instead of boils, and the full flavor of the tea is never released. So I can't really enjoy the splendid Kenyan tea until I get home, where the robust boiling water allows me to enjoy what is my favorite black tea.

My love affair with tea may have stemmed from my mother's frugality. I could get a good deal, the biggest food bargain anywhere. I can buy tea at the wildly high cost of $150 per pound and still pay only a few cents for each cup I brew. I can take ten trips to China, Africa and the Indian sub-continent for less than the price of a candy bar.

Though, just as you can't get a good cup of tea in the Kenyan highlands, it's near impossible to get good tea at even the best restaurants in America. The time and attention it takes to brew a good cup of tea isn't cost-efficient, so you get a tea bag and warm water brought to the table, or it's improperly prepared in the kitchen.

44

I've been spoiled all these years. I won't drink anything but good tea. This I turn into an advantage. I skip ordering a hot beverage altogether at the end of a restaurant meal and feel virtuous, having saved a few dollars.

I begin every morning quietly and slowly with a cup of brewed tea. I choose from among a half-dozen, some strong and astringent, some milder and smoother. In the afternoons I drink green, oolong, or jasmine. I love the color of the liquor as light is refracted through a glass cup, and I smell the rising steam. When I place a spoonful of the dark, powdered Kenyan tea in a warm pot, I think about the green fields of Kenya and my friends who grow tea there. I remember those who invited me into their homes and served bread and butter and tea from blue metal kettles. They drink theirs sweet and milky. They always prepared mine plain, no milk, no sugar—*turungi*, they say in Swahili, "true tea."

On summer days my grandchildren and I have tea parties in my backyard with a miniature porcelain teapot and its tiny cups and saucers. I want to introduce them to the pleasures of tea. This is the beverage of emperors and laborers, good only when made slowly and appreciated only when sipped. It is also cheap.

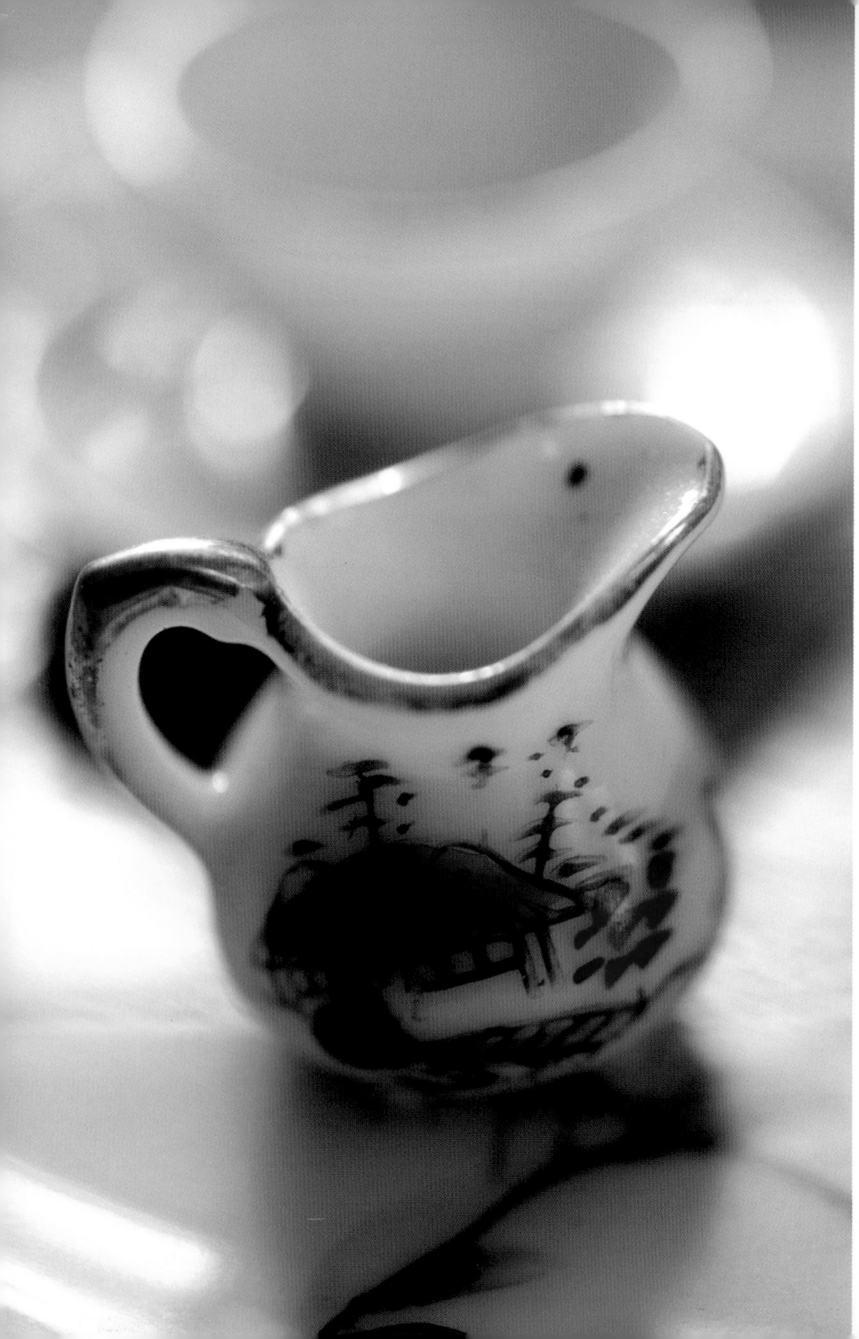

My life is ordered
around teapots and tea:
A morning pot for black,
an afternoon for green or oolong.
On the first day of summer
I take out two
appropriate for the season—
purple clay and one smaller.
To celebrate autumn
I use a pot the color
of fallen leaves,
and another unexpected bargain
bought at an art museum.
In winter I use sturdy pots,
presents brought back from Shanghai.
Those for spring are the loveliest,
shapes and swirls to touch and feel.
And there's one more—
for peach or jasmine or rose—
to use whenever I please,
an act of disorderly inspiration.

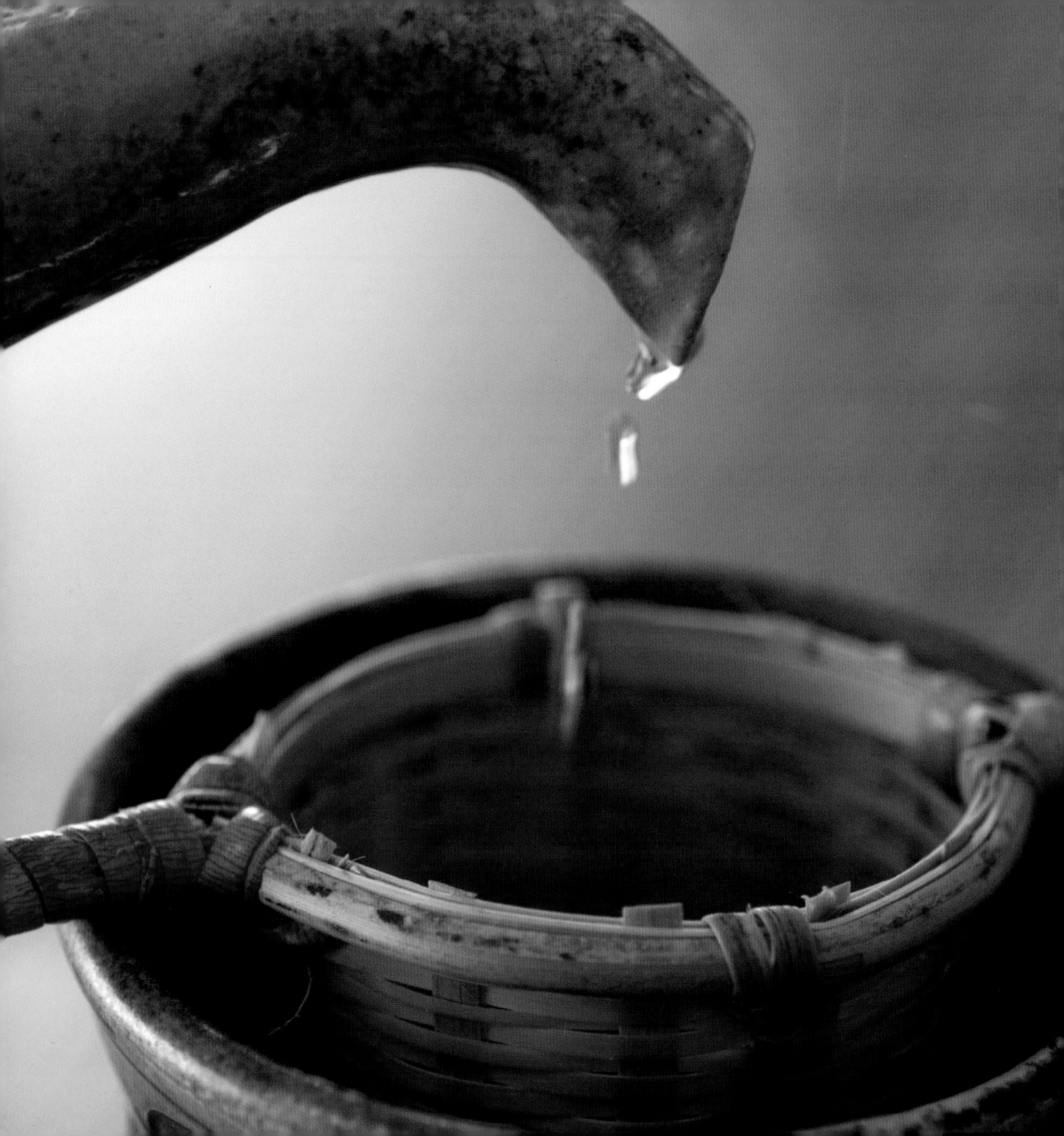

Kenya, Marinya Estate

by Marc E. Hofstadter

Dark fingers select delicate buds.
Leaves flutter on sun-parched savannas
and roots reach deep into ebony loam.
Blood flows in this liquid,
black plasma of our ancestors.

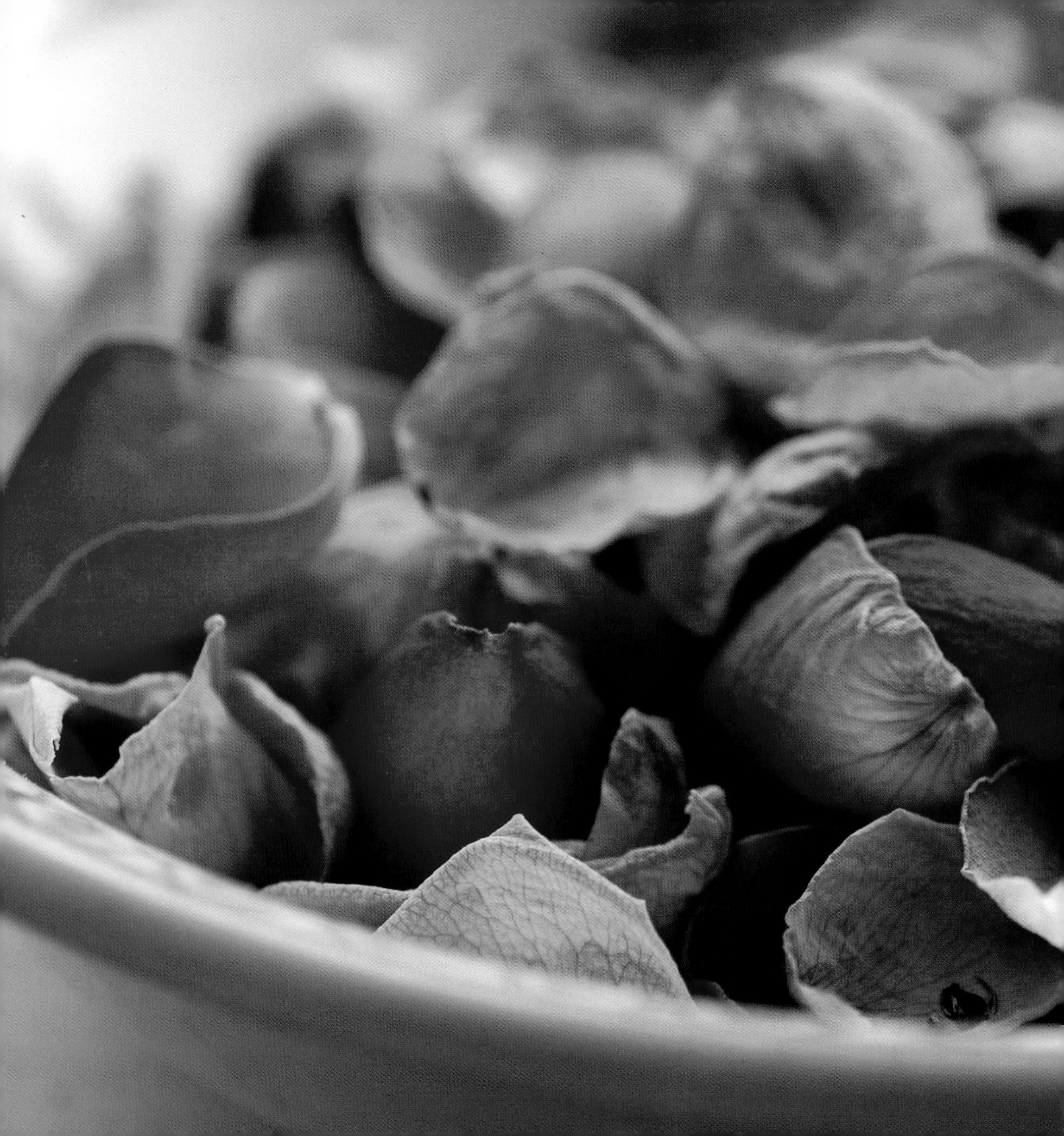

CHAI

by Saumya Arya Haas

Y ou can buy it already mixed, in a box. I was taught better, so I assemble the ingredients. Ginger, cardamom, cinnamon, nutmeg, butter, whole milk, dark brown sugar; these you can find anywhere. Then, from dark corners of the kitchen, I gather my precious spices: Kashmiri saffron, dried rose petals, fresh vanilla beans from Madagascar, long-cut Darjeeling stored in a silver tin.

I cut tough, fibrous ginger with a knife, leaving small puddles of juice soaking into the cutting board. A distinctive tang fills the air. I also use ginger for digestive problems and treatment for lung or sinus congestion. Like most roots, it is considered a male spice, and in magical use it is said to be good for reviving flagging passion and repressed grief.

But I am only making chai, Indian spiced tea, of which

there are limitless varieties. You can find it on any street corner in India. Sometimes it is called *Desi chai*, the tea of the country, and so it is. Amid the diversity of the teeming subcontinent, whether you are with proud desert dwellers, or in the steaming jungle of the South, or in the cool mountains or the sweating cities, anywhere in the unpredictable chaos of India you can count on a strong-brewed cup of sweet chai. If we have a national beverage, this is it.

I reach for the granite mortar and pestle I use to grind hard spices and dried roots. I pour light green cardamom from a smoky brown glass jar and begin to grind. I have a special love for the wrinkled, dry little pods. Cardamom is a female spice, a pod, the aroma thick, seductive. Like all feminine spices, it is bitter if not stored and treated properly, so I grind carefully. It's good for headaches and stimulating digestion, so I never let myself run out of cardamom.

Saffron is next. One of the most precious spices, the harvested stamens of this rare bloom are found in only a few parts of the world. I favor the deeper flavor of saffron grown in the valleys of Kashmir over the mass-produced product of Spain. I keep saffron in a small wooden box along with a mother-of-pearl mortar and pestle as big as my pinkie. Saffron is fickle, the queen of spices. Even in India, it is dear and difficult to find.

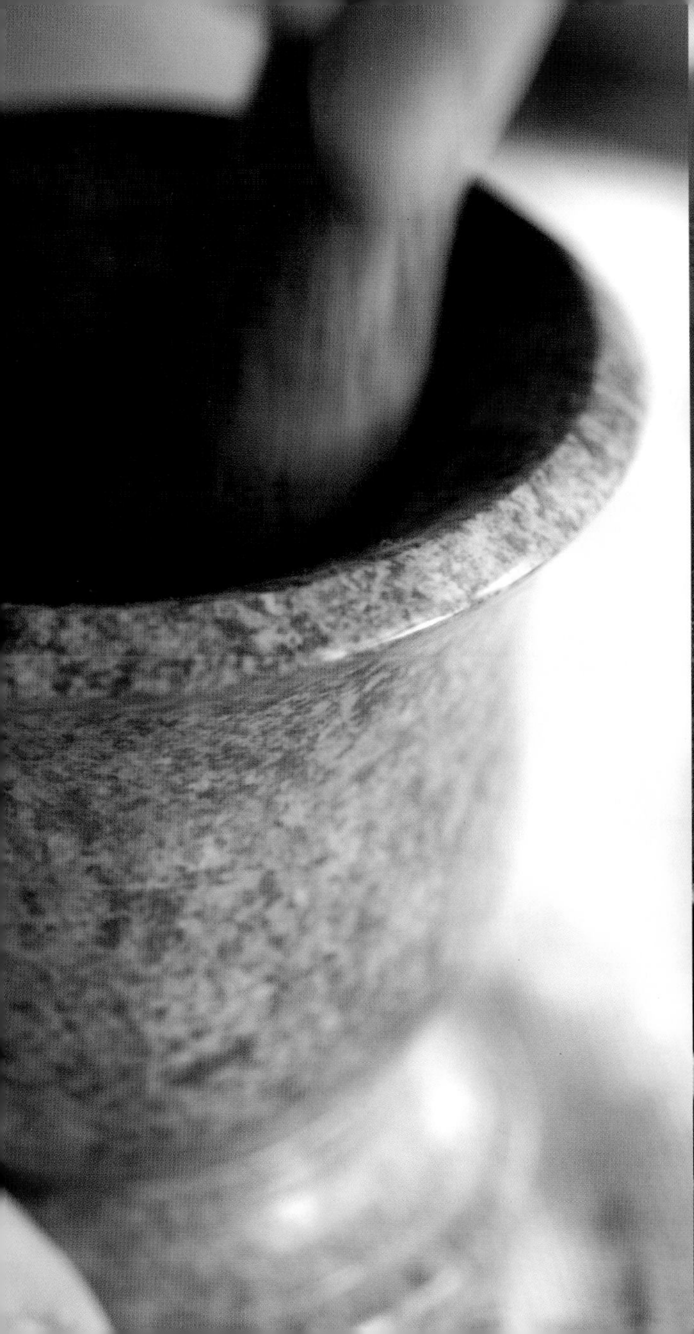
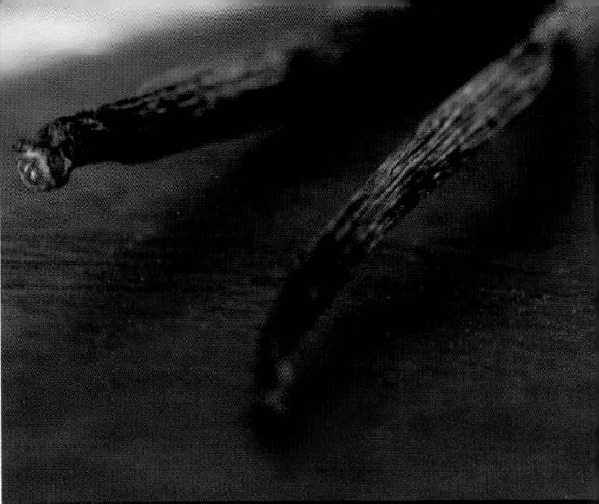
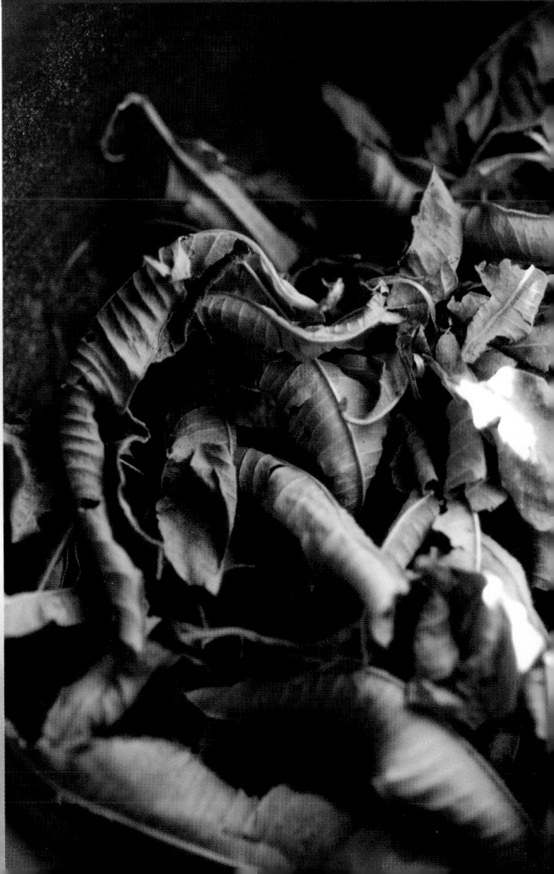

My nanny was the healer for her community, and often sent me into the woods collecting fresh herbs or into the market to buy dried spices. One day she told me the old spice seller was in the bazaar, and I should go see if she had any saffron.

"She's a funny old thing, some say mad, but her spices are the best. Don't pay any attention to the nonsense she talks, and if she won't sell anything to you, don't bother arguing. Sometimes she takes a dislike to people."

So I whistled for my dog and headed out to wander the market.

The old lady was easy to find. She was standing amid the clamor of the vegetable and spice market arguing with a harried vendor about the price of chilies. Her voice was strong, and I think she got the better of the chili seller. She wore a ragged sari, tied in the manner of the mountain gypsies, and carried a battered wooden box on her head. Her hair hung unbraided, gray and greasy, and she had an amazing number of pouches about her person. Bunches of plants dangled from her waist, not quite concealing a small, wickedly sharp-looking curved knife. Even amid the strong smells of the market, she exuded the scent of spices.

When she turned towards me, I found myself unaccountably

nervous under her steady gaze, the evenness of her expression at odds with her haggard appearance. I told her I wanted some saffron and she commenced digging through various bags without comment, finally producing a small bundle. When she quoted me a price her voice was low, surprisingly cultured. I handed over the money, took my purchase, and walked away disappointed, having looked forward to the ravings of a madwoman, and a story to tell later.

I smile to myself as I soak the bruised saffron in a small copper container of rose petals and warm water. I hadn't realized, all those years ago, that the tale would come later, as my nanny taught me how to make the tea I am making now: *Raj chai*, the royal tea.

This is the tale:

Long ago, deep in the secret heart of the mountains, lived a powerful man grown twisted. His magic kept his charges chained, bound with a spell that would burst their hearts within their chests if they deviated from the tasks set by their master. Though the magician had long ceased to age, his slaves lived short lives. They came to mean so little to him that he began breeding them like animals. Eventually the slaves forgot freedom and did not question their fate or fight the magician. In those days, the mysteries of herbs were known only to a

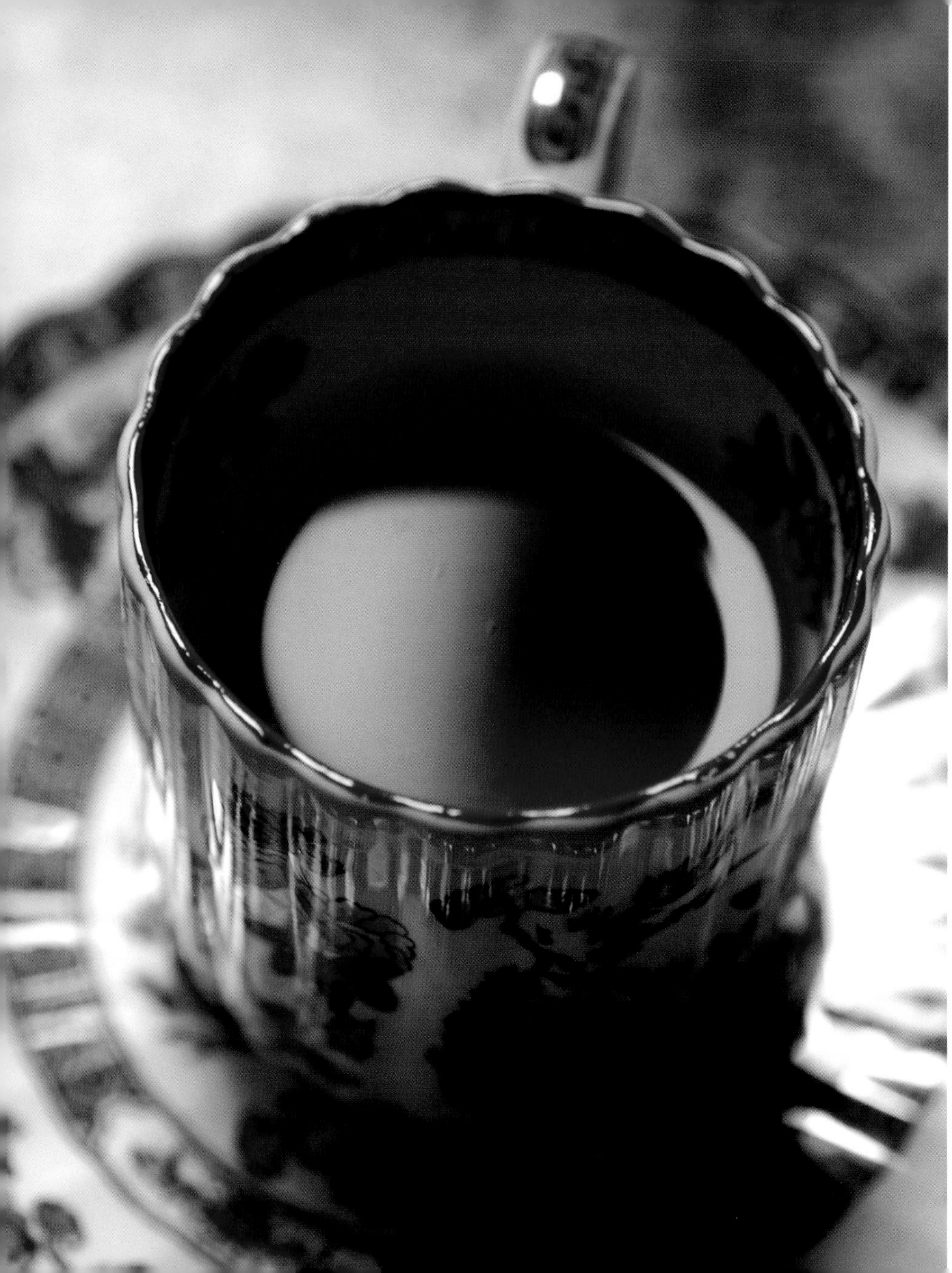

few. The mage sent his slaves deep into great shadowed jungles, across wasted deserts, to countries at the farthest borders of the world to find herbs. There was great peril in travel; many met violent ends from beasts of all manner, furred, feathered, and clean of skin.

For many years, the evil mage sought the herb Mandragora, the herb of true sight, which grew in the realm of the God Shiva himself. Some said Shiva's land was so wild with leopards that few ever returned. Others said (and still do) that the land high up among the glaciers would destroy the minds of those without pure hearts. Either way, none of the slaves ever survived this journey.

For centuries, the magician continued to grow in power without Mandragora. Many sought him for healing, but all were turned away, no matter how great their need. Then in the Year of Drought, on the dark night sacred to Shiva, a slave girl was born. She grew beautiful and strong, and there always seemed a peace about her. But she never spoke. When she entered a room, even the mage would grow unaccountably silent. She seemed insurmountable; any task he sent her on, any journey he put forth, she completed. When she grew into womanhood, the mage sent her far into the realm of the God, to bring back Mandragora if she could.

The young woman set out on her quest with a steady heart. What the mage did not know was that she had so grown to love the herbs she harvested that she spoke only to them. She wept when she had to cut them from the earth. As she journeyed to the mountain of Shiva, through forests of tall pines, over fields of bright flowers, she found a happiness stirring her heart that she had never felt before. As moons passed, the trail grew more arduous. She began to tire. When she passed out of the woods into the land of rock and sky, she grew ill with fatigue. Death trailed her footsteps. Finally, at the end of her endurance, she passed into the thin air of the ice fields of Shiva, high above the world. In the middle of the glacier, she fell to her knees exhausted.

With the last of her strength, she cried out in despair, not to her master, nor to the God, but to the spice for whose sake her life was ebbing from her. Suddenly, she saw in front of her a small, twisted root shaped like the body of a man with the head of the dragon— Mandragora, the spice of the God. She scooped it up with trembling fingers, unable to believe what she held. The herb spoke to her.

Child of slavery, why do you call me from my abode? Why do you seek to enslave me as you have been enslaved? I am the herb sprung from the tears Shiva wept when humankind discovered violence and hatred. Do not make me a tool of such, for it will break my spirit. Give me my freedom.

Hearing this, she could not bring herself to capture Mandragora; she placed it gently on the ground in silence. The herb, seeing the purity of her heart, spoke again.

Nameless child of slavery, I have seen into your heart, and know your thoughts. Because you released me, I will aid you. Complete your quest and bring me to the mage. I am the son of the God of Death and Healing, and on this journey I will dispense them both.

Knowing her task was nearly over gave the young woman strength. She wrapped the herb in her basket and began the long journey to the magician's keep.

The mage, shocked to see her return, instantly snatched the root and ran to his study. But nothing he could do, no spell or potion, would cause the herb to reveal its secrets. Finally, he cut it in half, rejoicing in its silent pain, and drank a tea made of the dragon head. The power of Mandragora is truth, and when the evil mage saw the blackness of his own heart, he withdrew his magic in remorse and fell to the floor, dead.

When the slaves found the lifeless body of their master, they became terrified, crying, "Who will care for us now?" The girl, weeping over the bleeding herb, comforted the other slaves, shocking them with the sound of her voice. She told them that they did not need their master, that freedom had come to them, and that they had great knowledge of herbs, needed by all. They would share their spices and knowledge and bring the ways of healing to all. None would abuse such power again.

So it came that these former slaves discovered freedom, and to honor this gift, they treated plants with respect, not enslaving them to tasks but speaking to them and asking their guidance. The Spice Mages began to travel, never staying long in one place. They harvested and sold the herbs of nourishment and healing, and they grew to great power themselves. In time, they became legend.

"It is said the old woman who sold you the saffron is one of them, a Spice Mage who knows all the mysteries. The mages are scattered now," my nanny told me, "and people have forgotten their story, for the world has moved on. But an echo of their legend survives for those of us who rely on blessings of the herbs and know a few of their secrets. That is why your mother will not cook if she is angry, why I scold you if you prepare tea remedies thoughtlessly. That is why your father does not eat food that is sold in boxes, and why you should not.

The knowledge that food heals is a gift."

I throw a pat of butter in the heated pan, and when it begins to sizzle I add the tea leaves. I stir once, wait until the leaves "bloom," releasing their fragrance, then add milk. The tea rolls to a boil immediately. Ginger and cardamom follow and, reducing the heat to a simmer, I thin the mixture with water and add the cinnamon, nutmeg, sugar, vanilla. After the tea boils again and I can smell the mingled scents of the spices filling my kitchen, I turn off the heat. Letting the tea cool for a few minutes, I put things away, my hands lingering on the familiar tools of my craft. I ponder the tale told to me long ago and the truth of it that I can grasp: the preparing of food, especially tea, is a blessing; the knowledge of healing has been handed down by countless generations.

Time for the last step, the true secret of *Raj chai*. When the tea is ready, I pour in saffron, rose petals, and the prayer of thanks that completes the recipe. I stand in the kitchen, listening for the spices.

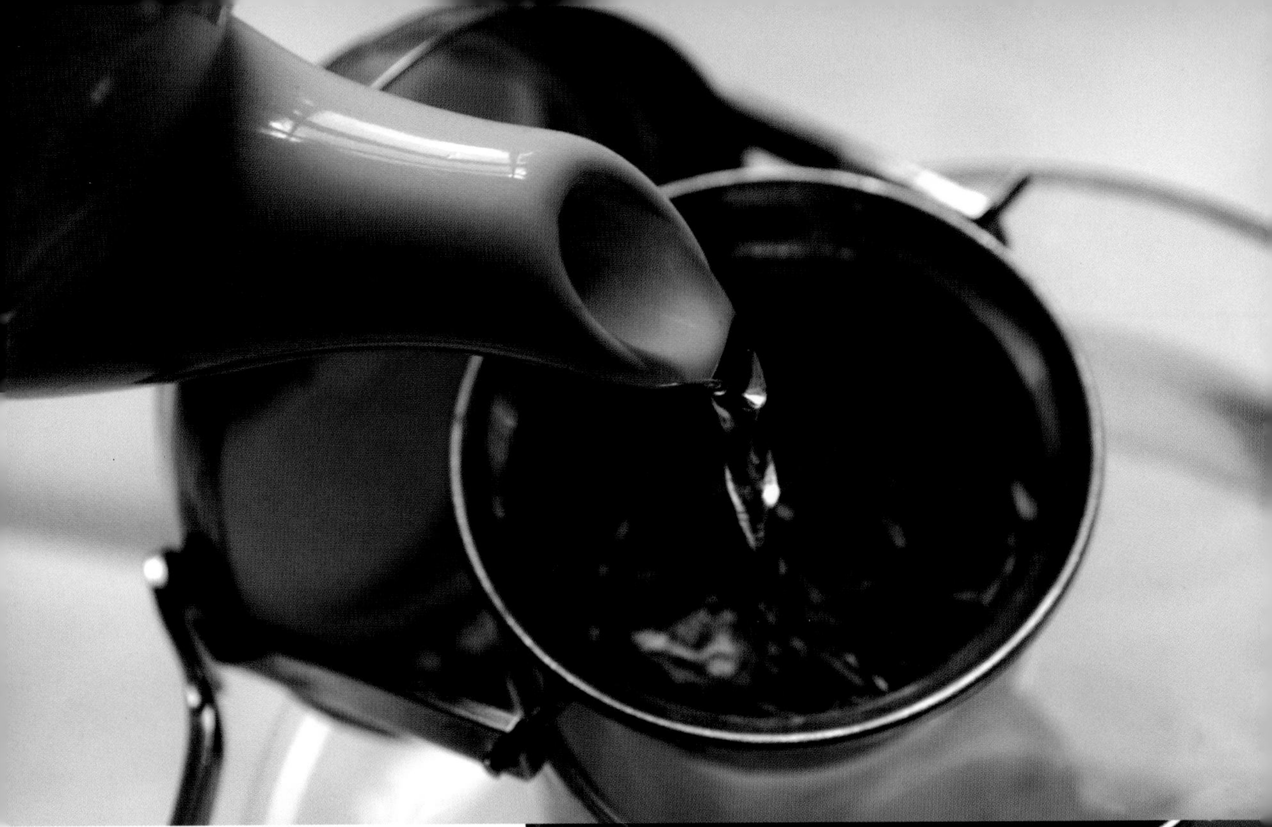

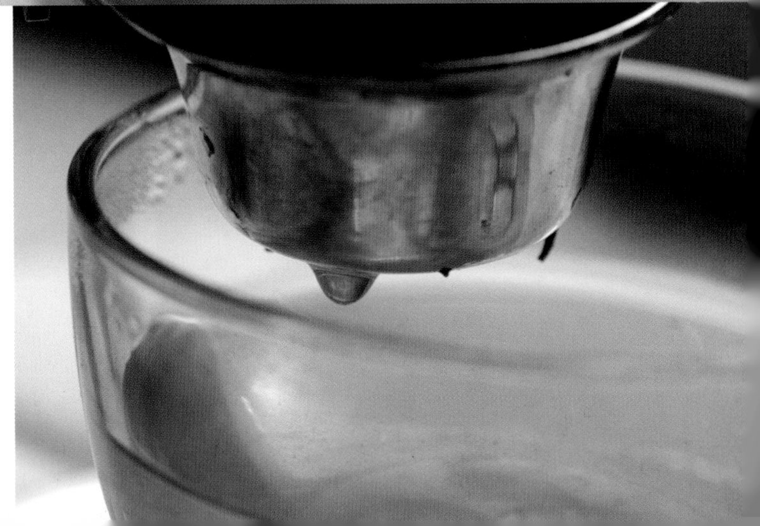

STREAMING GREEN TEA

by Sharon Bard

DESCENT

My guide walked me to the underground railroad station and handed me a piece of paper with the name of a railway stop in Urawa City. It was printed in Japanese, with an English transliteration next to it. She gave me several coins and pushed me down the steps to the gate. I turned to ask her a question but she was gone.

It was 1977. I was on a tour of five Asian countries. My special education director in California had once hosted a Japanese man doing an internship in the United States. This gentleman was returning the gesture, and I was to spend the night with his family, thousands of miles from home.

In that dark underground, there were no reference points to connect with: no sky, mountains, or apartment buildings. Swarms of Japanese hovered on the platform, standing very close, speaking an indecipherable language. Lots of vowels, "ee" and "ah" sounds. As the train approached, they rushed to the doors, and the backs of my knees began to shake. Quite simply, I was scared. I entered a metal car and with a jerk, we took off into blackness. My panic escalated.

The train speeded along in no discernible direction, past signs printed in Japanese. The announcer called out stops but I couldn't understand him. I had no idea what Mr. Mochizuki, the man I was to meet, looked like. Nor did I know the value of the coins clutched in my hand along with the name of the transliterated station. I did have a phone number for the modest hotel in Tokyo, miles away, where my group was staying. But I didn't know how to use a phone. For those twenty minutes under the ground, speeding somewhere, in the heart of the Orient, I was terribly disoriented.

From the speaker overhead I heard a few syllables that sounded as if they might belong to the name of my stop. With a leap of faith and a tug on the cord, I signaled my exit. As the car whizzed into the station I was able to match the letters on the wall with those in my sweaty palm. I grabbed my overnight bag, and with shaky knees, walked out of the car.

I was the only Western woman exiting the train amid a sea of Asian faces. Mr. Mochizuki had no trouble recognizing me. He bowed deeply, then shook my hand awkwardly, as if an afterthought. His warm smile and that small hint of his vulnerability were comforting.

"I am so very pleased meeting you. My family they want to meet you too. But I am too sorry for this. My wife she has cold and must wear mask. We cannot allow you to our home for fear you too would be sick with cold. I must take you to hotel."

The hotel was small and rather sterile. I did not know how to order dinner. A woman brought a pot of hot, green tea to my room. I sipped it slowly, letting fluid and warmth permeate fatigued muscles. I let it slow my breath. It tasted sharp, almost but not quite bitter. I was alone in a strange room in a city near Tokyo, sitting on an orange and white quilt with stylized butterflies. Still anxious, but with a renewed sense of adventure, I unpacked my bag, soaked in a deep tub, and fell into an even deeper sleep.

65

CONNECTION

Mr. Mochizuki met me in the lobby at 7:00 A.M. We had a quick breakfast of rice and eggs. "You are sleeping well ?" he asked.

"Yes, thank you."

"We will go to school first. I am principal. You will meet students and officials. After I will show you city, then put you in cab for Tokyo." I thanked him and bowed. He paid the bill and we got into his car.

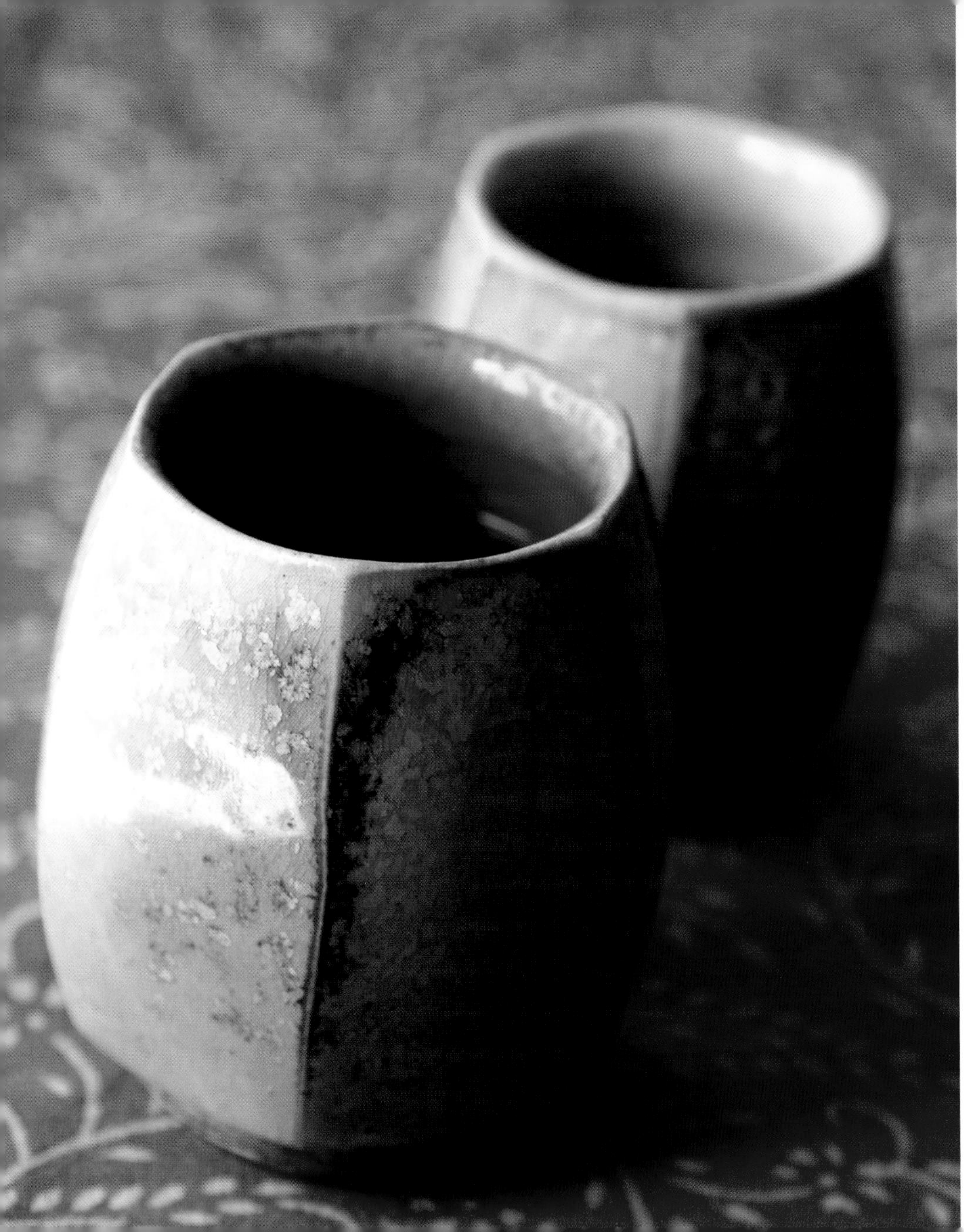

We passed apartment buildings and cows on the short drive from the little hotel to the school. He parked in a space toward the front door. "My spot," he told me with a grin. I smiled, pulled out a camera, took a picture of the school. At the entryway were rows of black slippers.

"These for you," he said, handing me a pair and grabbing a larger set for himself. I placed my tan loafers on the shelf and entered the lobby, my feet adjusting to slick rubber soles.

"Please come to office," he said, escorting me down the hall. We entered his room and he ushered me to a low foam couch.

"We will drink tea first," he explained. Mr. Mochizuki walked behind a bamboo screen and reappeared with a tray of hot tea. Sitting down, he deftly poured us each a cup, and began to talk to me.

"I am work hard to understand these students. I write two books, which I gift to you. One is about curriculum, other is philosophy. Maybe some day you learn to read Japanese." Big smile. He brought the books to me.

I was warmed by his kindness and the tea. Despite unfamiliar smells and sights, and although I was sitting across from a total stranger, I felt comfortable. Mr. Mochizuki was respectful, not only toward me, but in the ritual of sharing his sweet, green tea.

"Please sign your books for me," I asked, and he did. I thanked him, took another photo, practiced another bow. He then put my cup back on the tray.

"Now is time for tour," he told me. "You will see students, what you call trainable retarded. They don't read or write. We teach them simple tasks. They will work. Earn modest salary."

Mr. Mochizuki walked me gingerly through the spotless corridors in his special school, both of us wearing our black slippers. We went to a classroom where a teacher had lined up two dozen youngsters for roll call. They were between eight and ten years old, all wearing blue and green cotton uniforms. Five Yamaha organs and a giant trampoline filled most of the floor. As we entered the doorway, the teacher glanced toward us, lines of distress etched into her brow and along the sides of her mouth. She lowered her eyes not so much in reverence as in shame. In the corner of the room, one of her students was hanging upside down on a bookcase, his little blue and green torso swinging gently. Mr. Mochizuki said something to the teacher, smiled to me, and uttered in lilting English, "Hy-per-ac-TIVITY!"

PURPOSE

We observed several more classrooms brimming with blue and green cotton. There were young children bent over pegboards, others trying to copy letters of their names using thick pencils. Young adults pushing brooms. Active. Intent. I'd seen these activities repeatedly; the uniformity of mental retardation transcended national boundaries.

Mr. Mochizuki looked at his watch. "It is time for our meeting," he told me, and we turned down another corridor and into a small conference room. Three men in business suits were seated at a dark wooden table. They immediately rose from their chairs and bowed to me. After rapid, intense dialogue in Japanese, I was invited to take a seat. The man to my right poured us each a cup of green tea from a steaming metal teapot.

Mr. Mochizuki introduced the men to me, and they bowed again as if I were a dignitary. Was this a custom with foreigners, or women, or had my new acquaintance decided to capitalize on my visit in order to impress his superiors?

"My colleagues, they know you work hard in America with these children. We wish to know the things you do that make big difference, even small change. Our country is slower to notice handicaps. For educating."

More smiles. All eyes were on me. I put down my tea cup. It was time to talk.

"I, too, am a principal of a small school for severely handicapped students. Most of our pupils are more disabled than the children here," I began, enunciating slowly. Mr. Mochizuki translated.

"We had hospitals for children like these in California. But then our governor signed laws for them to leave the hospitals and go back into the community. In part to save money."

Translation into Japanese. Nods.

"Now there is a movement to include these students in regular programs. Into a less restrictive environment. So they can have equal education. We call it mainstreaming."

More translation.

"Please say it again."

"Mainstreaming."

Notebooks opened. A Pilot Razor pen appeared and one of the men carefully inscribed that Western buzzword into neat little ideographs.

"Main steaming," said another. Two of the men looked at me. The third looked over to the flat teapot, connecting my term with the escaping vapors.

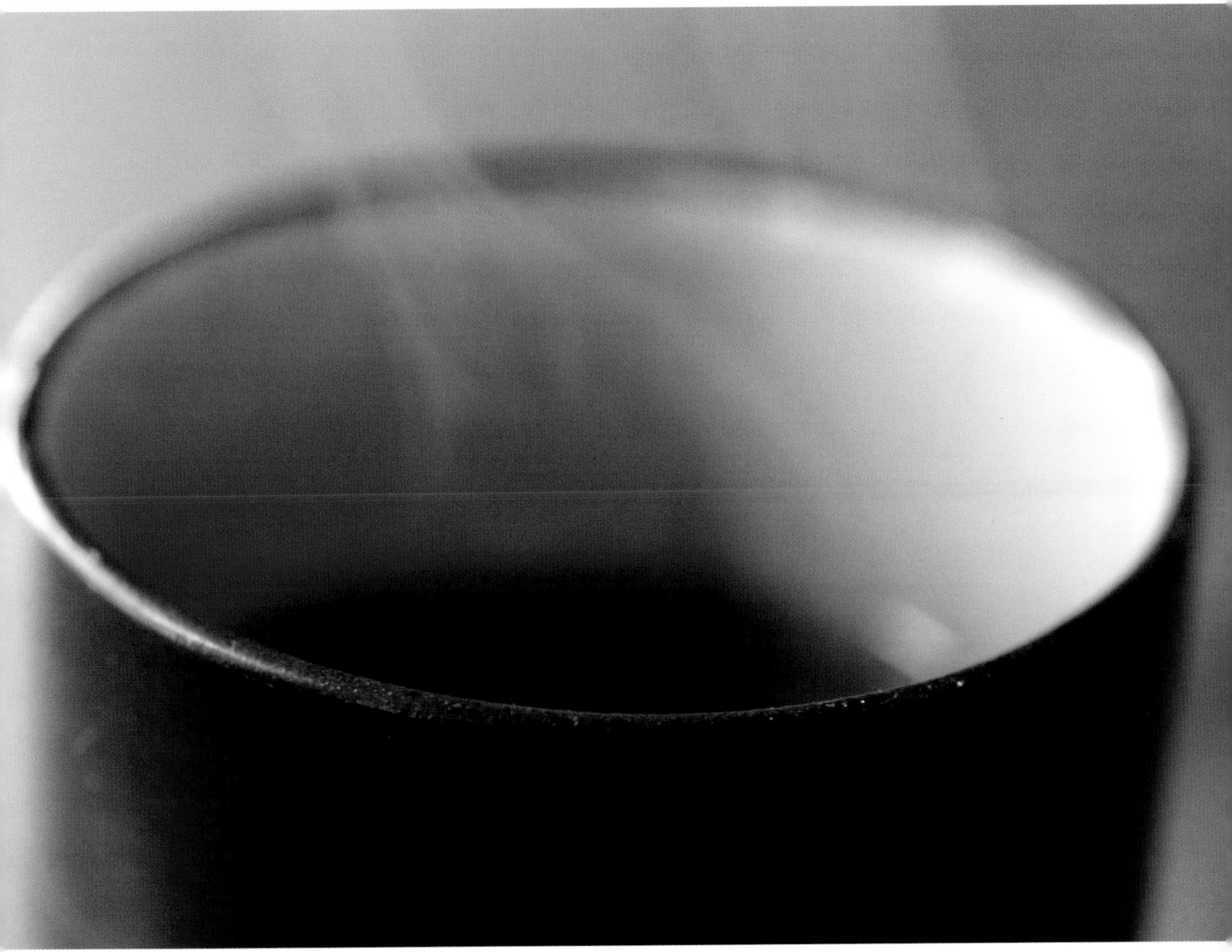

"Main STREAM ing, I repeated. "Stream, small river."

"Main st-leaming," they replied in unison.

Smiles. Nodding. The meeting was over. Mr. Mochizuki poured more of the green tea. This brew wasn't as sweet. The men chatted excitedly.

"We will now use your new term in our teaching. In our books. It is a good word. Main st-leaming. St-reaming. Thank you for new concept."

How important I felt in that moment. International ambassador for the disabled. The fate of ten thousand mentally retarded Japanese students rested on my information. Kids might be moved from the familiar Yamaha organ and trampoline territory into regular classrooms. Stiffer competition. I had seen the drawbacks of a mainstreamed curriculum. Fiscal cutbacks were underneath the equal education rhetoric. In the last ten years, only one student at my school had been capable of moving into a more normal environment. Would it work any better in Japan, where there was such pressure to conform?

I took another sip of tea. And smiled. Caution behind the smile. I was riding the wave of importance. The men rose, we bowed, and Mr. Mochizuki brought me back to his office to pick up the books.

RETURN

"I show you our city now," he told me. I followed him down the hall and to the front lobby where I retrieved my shoes. We drove past homes, small shops and parks.

"Paper fish means boy's birthday," he told me, pointing to a bright carp waving in the breeze. "And good luck. We stop here."

We strolled down a commercial street in the outskirts of Urawa City. People walked briskly, purposefully, especially the elders. The windows of the storefronts were filled with colorful gadgets. He bought me a burgundy silk satchel to carry the books. "A memento of Japan," he told me. We had one last cup of tea in a sushi shop. The prices were

high. An electric Kirin beer sign winked at me.

I held the small ceramic mug between my fingers and looked across the table at Mr. Mochizuki. He looked tired. We smiled. Questions formed inside my head. Was my visit helpful? Could he share a concept I could take back to America? But these inquiries did not make their way to my voice. It suddenly seemed too hard to talk. I would soon be back in Tokyo with the other Americans. I swallowed the last of the tea. It had not steeped very long, and tasted thinner than the school tea. Slightly bitter. "I am very grateful for your hospitality," I told him, not knowing what etiquette errors I might have made.

We bowed. He walked me to the corner and hailed a cab. We bowed again, said goodbye. I entered the back seat of the taxi, satchel at my side, impressions of the overnight journey steeping within.

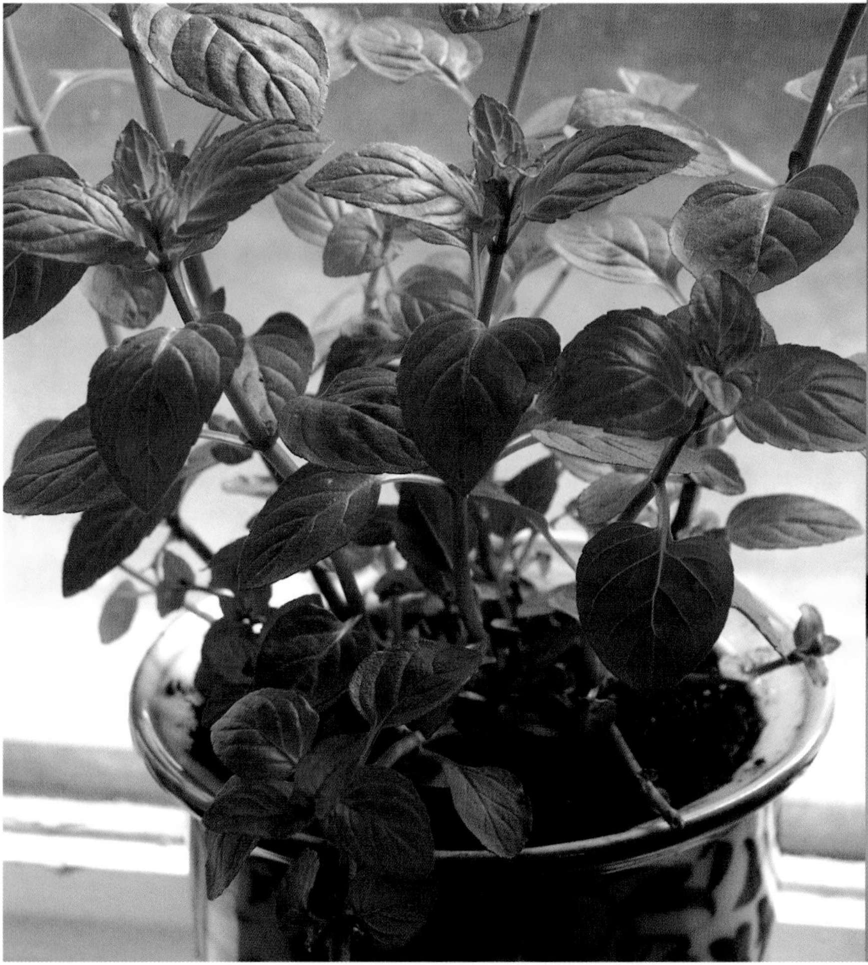
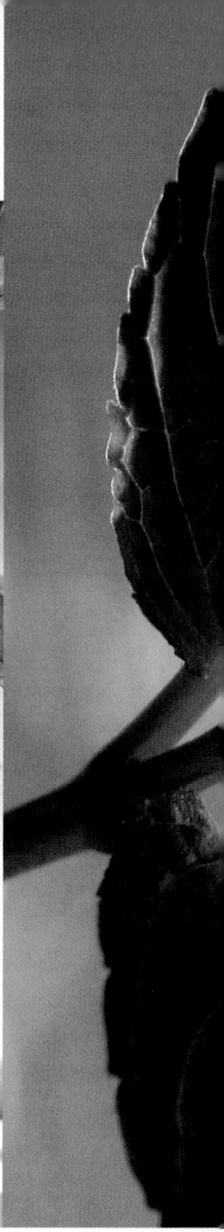

Peppermint Tea:
A Cultural Inheritance
Savoring the Quiet Moments

by Susan Muaddi Darraj

The process of buying a house is intense: stressful, but exciting. When we moved into our new home, my husband and I were eager to put our mark on it. One of the first items on my agenda was a small herbal garden. We contemplated which plants we wanted to grow. "Definitely peppermint," I said. "For our tea." He smiled. I knew he understood the significance of my suggestion. *Shay ma' naa'-naa'* (tea with peppermint) is a staple in our lives. Everyone drinks tea in our culture, including young children (and nobody worries about caffeine excess). Sipping hot tea, watching the fresh peppermint leaves sink to the bottom of your cup in the company of friends and family, reflects the Middle Eastern spirit of community.

But I grew up watching my parents drink coffee and only came to love tea later. In the mornings, in our south Philadelphia row house, my mother—who had a day filled with four unruly children awaiting her—refused to stir unless she heard the coffee pot dripping and sizzling, just like the Folger's commercial. My father worked two or three jobs in those days; he needed his thick, black liquid, too. Stress was high. My parents had a sizeable mortgage and only one salary since my mother had left her job to raise the family. It was understood that my brothers and I would wear hand-me-downs from our older cousins and not complain, just as it was understood that we were not to push my father for a piggy-back ride around the living room if he looked especially haggard and weary (he would do it just to please us and wake up with a backache the next morning). My childhood memory of the gentle, reassuring sound of the coffee maker in the morning is co-mingled with memories of the fatigue that marked those days.

I rarely saw my parents drink tea, although I knew that my mom kept a jar of dried peppermint leaves for special occasions when we had guests and tea was required. Tea was the "weaker" drink, the "un-coffee," in my childish understanding, because it lacked the robustness and soldier-like, rugged quality of strong, black American coffee. When I started college and then graduate school, I dismissed tea as inadequate for the quick pace of my daily schedule, turning naturally to coffee to help me make it through exams and term papers, as I had seen my parents rely on it all my life.

When I was twenty-two years old, though, my attitude changed. I spent the summer in Palestine, visiting my paternal grandmother and aunt and taking classes in Arabic at the local university. There, tea was a regular habit, as ritualistic as the muezzin's call from the mosque in the nearby village, or the bells tolling from the church tower in our own. My aunt and I boiled water and made tea for breakfast, lunch, and dinner, as well as for the frequent times when neighbors and guests would drop in for a visit. Offering tea to one's guests was a routine as natural and as socially embedded as shaking their hands and inviting them to sit down.

The college cafeteria in Palestine was also dominated by tea. The penultimate feature of a Palestinian cafeteria line, before the cash register, was the stand of coffee and tea canisters. The tea was plain, but after you paid for the food, you headed for the condiments stand, where a box of raw sugar (impaled with a small spoon) and a batch of fresh, wet peppermint leaves awaited you. I spent many days in the cafeteria during lunch breaks, my Arabic grammar book propped open in front of me. I could barely bring myself to open to the chapter on verb tenses or *tashkeel* (vowel sounds) unless a cup of hot tea sat in front of me, spreading its minty, crisp aroma like inspiration.

Another lesson I learned that summer was that in Palestine, coffee assumed a different connotation from the wake-up-to-Folgers one it had in the States. Palestinians drink coffee on more serious occasions, such as weddings and funerals. When my friend announced that she'd met the man she wanted to marry, a formal meeting took place at her parents' home. The men from her side of the family sat in the living room beside her father and listened to the men from the future groom's side as they asked for my friend's hand. Before them were tiny, delicate, gold-plated cups filled with thick, black coffee, untouched until the discussion was complete. I knew that it had been sweetened because I was in the kitchen and had watched the women stir sugar into it as it boiled. When the betrothal was official, the men shook hands, kissed each other's cheeks, and drank their coffee.

That coffee had been made sweet for a happy occasion. At the

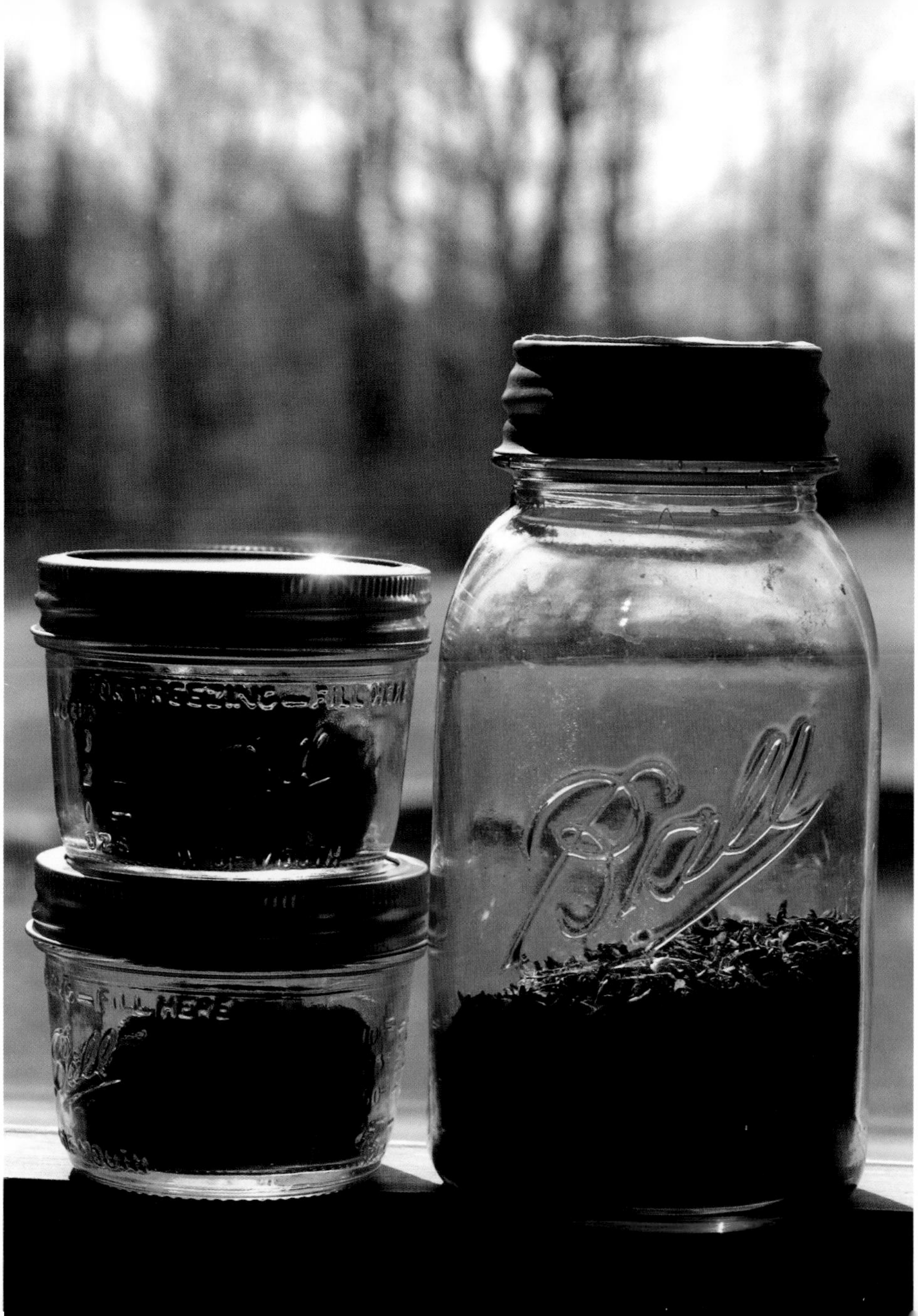
Ball

memorial mass for my grandmother forty days after her death, though, the coffee served was bitter. It had been prepared without sugar to mark the solemnity of the occasion. I sipped it appreciatively, for its taste paralleled my bitter and raw emotions.

Thus I came to associate coffee with the serious and dramatic events in life as well as with tedious chores and a grueling work schedule. But tea is different—tea is for the quiet moments in life when we have a rare glimpse of true happiness and satisfaction. It's a healer, an antidote for a number of ailments, including headaches, stomach aches, colds, and fatigue, and it heals on the emotional level as well. It's the glue that holds families and friendships together.

Long talks with good friends are always mediated with peppermint tea. To offer someone a cup is to invite them to share a story or giggle like a child or cry into your shoulder. It was over a cup of tea, as I inhaled the minty aroma, that I found out that my friend was seeking a divorce, that another's mother was quite ill, and that a third wanted to return to school and start her life over.

The boiling of water and infusion of tea leaves with peppermint takes me back to those quiet afternoons in Palestine, at my grandmother's house and in the college cafeteria, times when I paused in my day to reflect. The sensation of a hot ceramic mug in my hands and the smell of the fresh mint arising from within it offered me a rare chance to think. I appreciated the refreshing flavor of cup after cup that summer, as I read the reports in the papers that the peace process was slowly falling apart. Sometimes, as I pondered the future of a Palestinian state and recalled all that the Palestinians had endured in their history, I would feel so ill that a soothing cup of tea was the only thing I could stomach. I did a lot of thinking about my own life and my goals, about where I was headed and what I needed to do to get there. I realized that my life back in the United States was a stream of successive days that flowed together like waves, rippling and flowing over one another, each one indistinct and without special meaning. Over tea, I began to understand the value of self-reflection.

There have been moments in the process of getting married, moving to a new city, and buying a new home that have required coffee only: when we were creating the seating arrangements for our wedding reception ("No, Aunt Aida hates Uncle Nader," and "Cousin Amanda has been angry with Cousin Walid since last summer—they can't sit together!"); when I needed to find a job and would stay up late, poring over the help wanted ads and writing cover letters to

accompany customized resumes; and when I found out I'd have to be practically re-baptized to join and be married in my husband's church.

But tea moments have been more frequent and more pleasant. Tea is for when my in-laws come to visit and to check on our quickly blooming garden, and we end up talking and laughing about the family, or when a new friend I have made in the neighborhood stops by to say hello. It's for when I wake up in the middle of the night, worried about something unresolved, and I sit at the kitchen table with a hot cup of tea and think it out. When I sneak down to my study to write in my journal, savoring an undisturbed hour with a cup at my side and a pen in my hand. When another disturbance develops in the Middle East, and I see the names of people and places that I personally recognize in the morning paper. It's for when my husband and I sit down for long talks, and I learn something new about him that makes me love him even more.

It is springtime now and we have been in the house for only a few months. The first green is showing in my peppermint pot. Soon, I will be able to pick some leaves and drop them into a pot of water boiling on the stove. I look forward to long, pensive, summer afternoons on the porch of our new home, drinking in reflection, drinking in satisfaction.

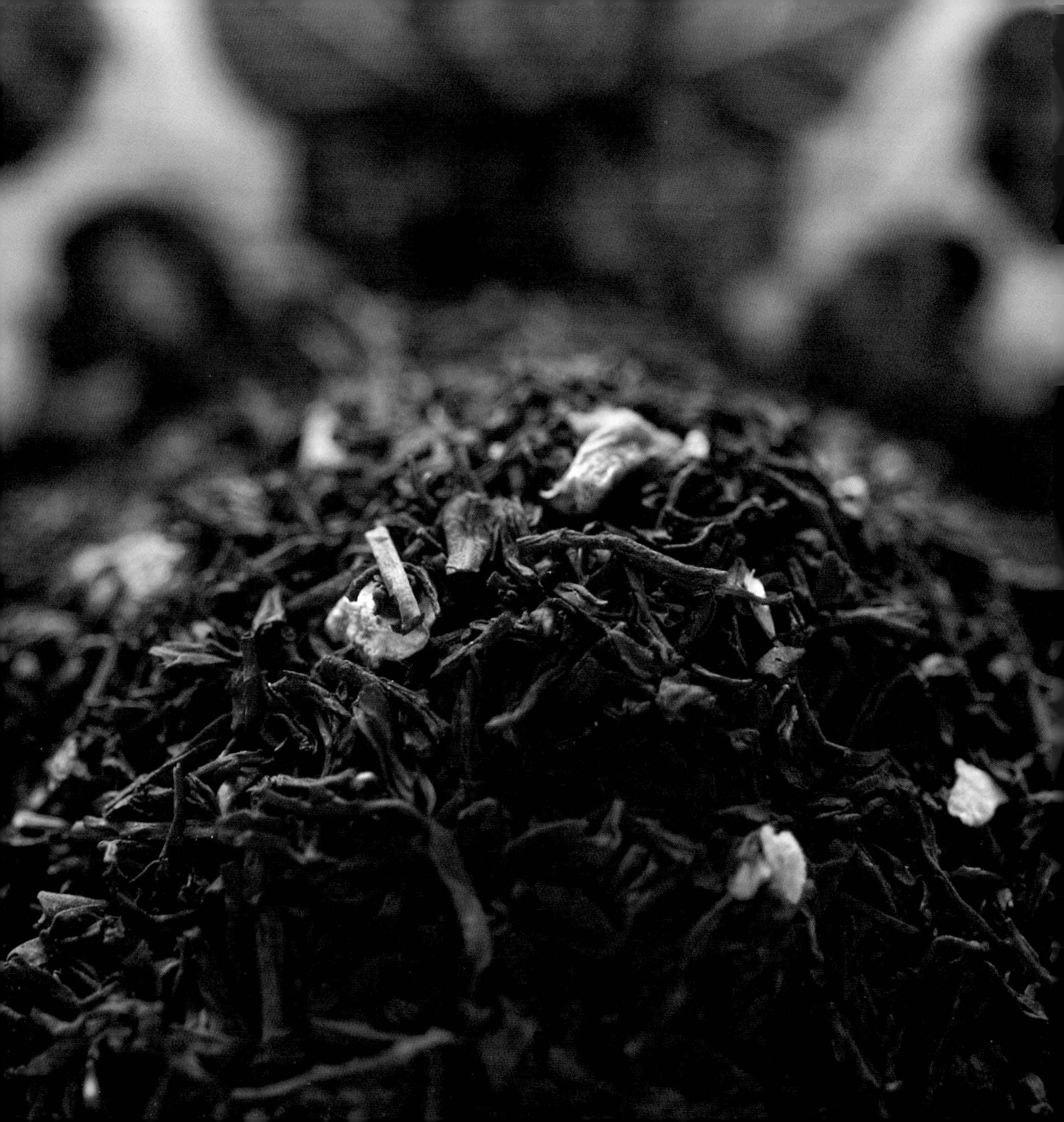

STRONG BREW

by Clara Rosemarda

My father and I shared a love of tea and adventure. His life of adventure was thwarted in his early twenties, but his love of tea remained steady throughout his life, as has mine.

In one of the earliest and strongest memories of my childhood, I am five years old, sitting with my family at our old mahogany dining room table, a small chandelier illuminating us. My Russian parents are drinking their tea from glasses; the thin gold rims give us a sense of prosperity. To keep the glass from cracking Dad places a spoon in it as he pours the hot brew. I am sipping tea from a saucer, strong black tea with lemon. With my tiny hands I lift the saucer, blow on the hot liquid and slurp.

My father's childhood memories were very different from mine: at the age of five, he saw another child speared to death in the 1903 Kishinev pogrom. At twenty he left his town in Bessarabia. With a sense of adventure and the fire of revenge burning in him, he went

Palestine to join the Jewish Legion. Although he was too short for their regulations, he managed to get in anyway. "I stood on my toes when they measured me," he told us with a sense of pride. "I needed to be three inches taller."

Eventually he emigrated to the States with his family and discovered the excitement of New York. Driven by a strong intellect and artistic talents, he enrolled in night school to become a dentist. But instead of the success he had dreamed of, he ended up working in a factory and nursing his ill mother. He dropped out of school when he found himself too tired to stay awake in class.

Getting married and having children ultimately added to his burdens. His disappointment with life in the "new country" began to oppress his natural sense of adventure. The family's move across the country to Los Angeles didn't help. His discontent, like a slow-moving storm, built into an anger that crashed unpredictably onto the shores of our daily life and left us quiet and fearful. But teatime was a break in the storm, a reliably good time for our family. That's when Dad planted himself firmly into the center of family life. The arguing and blame subsided. His quick temper, and even quicker tendency to criticize, dissolved in the sweet amber liquid.

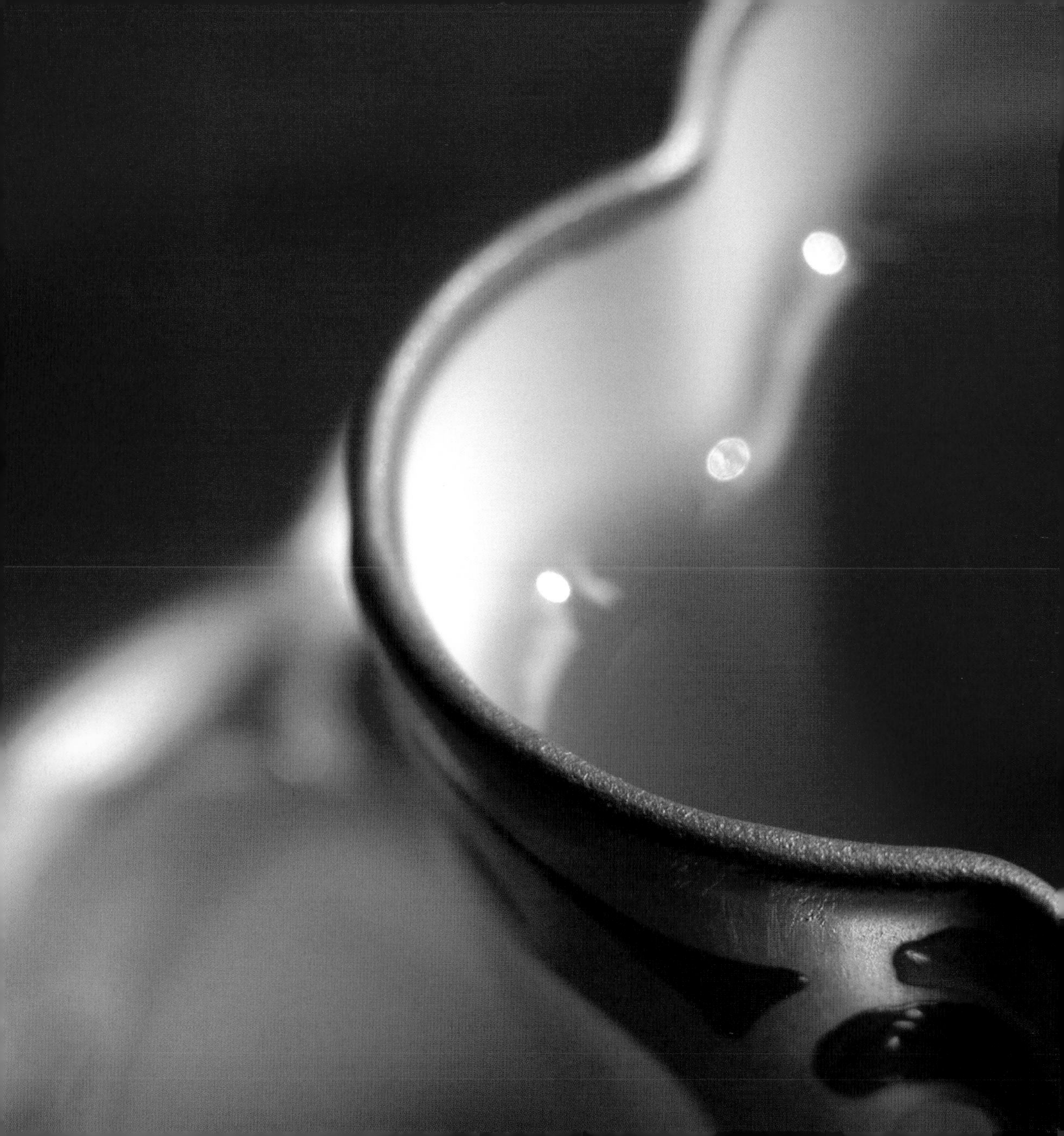

My parents settled into their rich soothing drink with a pleasure that brought out their personal warmth. I can still hear the clinking of spoons touching glass as they stirred their tea. They had landed. Teatime was not a filler between two important events; it was its own destination.

When they took those first sips, perhaps they settled into happy memories of drinking black tea from a family samovar, perhaps they saw reflections of themselves in my brother and me, perhaps they carried from Russia the simple ability to sit down and relax. Wherever they journeyed in those few moments, they provided me a precious peacefulness as we sipped together.

But those special times were rare; the old-world lifestyle was stifling and out of time. The sense of adventure I inherited from my father impelled me to move on. When I left our West Hollywood apartment for Manhattan, I carried with me my father's love for New York and his ritual of drinking tea. I searched in dimly lit Jewish grocery stores on First Avenue for the loose Swee Touch Nee tea in the red and gold tin box my parents had used in the past. Swee Touch Nee brought back the flavor of my life at home, a life I had left behind like an old love. The ritual of tea still brings back the rhythm and tone of those early days around the family table, times I now recall in a golden luminescence that only memory can create.

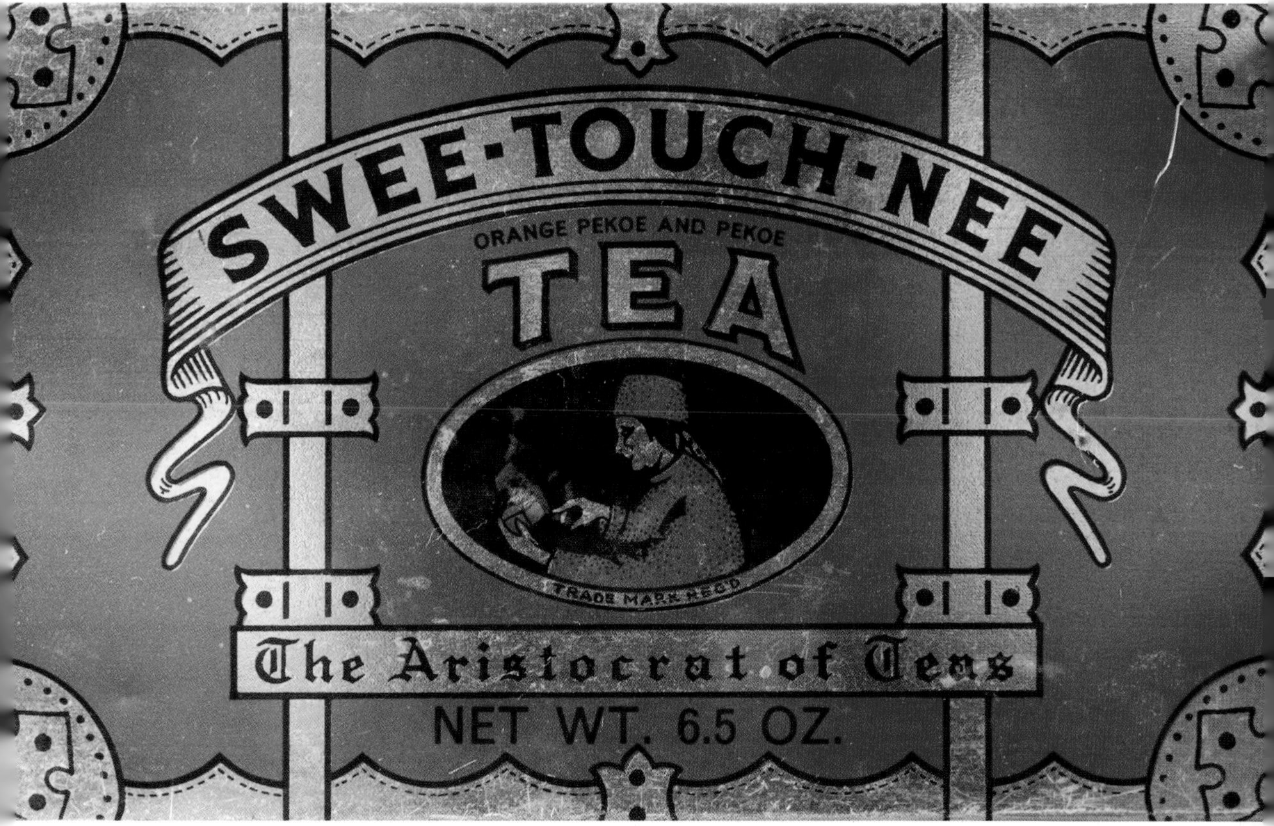
SWEE·TOUCH·NEE
ORANGE PEKOE AND PEKOE
TEA
TRADE MARK REG'D
The Aristocrat of Teas
NET WT. 6.5 OZ.

In New York I explored one of my father's old haunts, drawn there by the many stories he had told when I was growing up about his early days in Manhattan as a new immigrant. In his bachelor years, he had frequently stopped for tea and political discussions with his fellow countrymen at the east 14th street automat. "They would order a cup of tea in a glass with a lot of milk," he said of some of his comrades, smiling at the image conjured in his mind. Telling these stories, he re-entered the automat and mingled once again for those few moments with his old buddies from years earlier.

I discovered that a few men of my father's age and country still gathered at the same automat for tea and heated discussions. I gained new insight into my father's past by watching, and sometimes talking, to those old men. I could see who they were more clearly than I had ever seen my own father. They patted each other on the back, knew each other's names and, of course spoke Yiddish, an intimate language, as they sat around hugging their cups. They had found a kind of community in the cafeterias of New York where they could reminisce about the "old country." Yet, as my father had told me, these men only saw each other over tea. If one of them stopped coming the others might sit around wondering: Did he get married? Did he move? Did he die? They continued talking and drinking as if trying to solve a philosophical problem, but they made no effort to find out what really happened to their "landsman."

While sitting around small tables conversing in their own language, those immigrant men were held together by an invisible net that dissolved once they left the cafeteria. For the time they communed over tea their disparate lives floated harmoniously on the same waves. Once they walked out the door and into the streets of New York they were on their own, again strangers swimming in foreign waters.

This was also true in certain ways of my father and me. In the early days we could sit together discussing ideas, but once I walked out the door and started on my own adventures we became strangers. His dream for me was to marry, have a family and live nearby. My need to explore, so much like his own early longing, became even stronger as his world continued to narrow. He said very little and I kept my true feelings secret. I was finally breaking free. And yet all the while I was following his old dream.

In 1967, I traveled through Europe for several months with the man I would eventually marry. I journeyed by ship from Naples to Israel, the country my father had helped create, where I went to study

93

Hebrew and work on a kibbutz. Unlike the New York cafeteria Jews, members of the kibbutz not only worked together, they lived together. In the "old country," life was based on the past. But the kibbutz was modern; it was about the here and now. You were measured not by what you thought or said, not even by the job you had, but by the quality of your work and your enthusiasm for it, whether you shoveled cow-dung or taught in the children's school.

My father was a proud worker. He would have fit in well on a kibbutz. He wanted to return to Israel, but it was I who found my way there in my early twenties, the age when he stopped traveling and settled down. Dad would have loved the communal meals in the *chadar ha ochel*, the kibbutz dining hall, where we filed in from work and systematically filled the rows of tables from one end of the room to the other. Each table had the same staples: salt, pepper, sour pickles, salad, bread and a small stainless steel teapot with a concentrated brew of black tea that was usually tepid. The kibbutzniks were workers and farmers; they did not linger. They ate a hearty meal quickly, and then drank their tea the way Americans drink beer: they gulped it down, unconcerned with its temperature, and then returned to work.

The six months I spent on the kibbutz—working in the chicken coops, gathering eggs, digging trenches or hiding in them in the white desert heat—exploded my narrow, youthful vision of reality. My mind cracked open to something bigger and broader that allowed me to embrace others in a way my father and his cafeteria buddies never could. I felt more alive on the kibbutz than I had ever felt before.

There I was in a "new country," in 1967, anticipating a war, building trenches side by side with the kibbutzniks, watching the men being called away, one by one, to defend their country. I was in the midst of what would become a historical turning point in the Middle East, the Six Day War. I was young, in love, and taken in by the rolling wave of life, swimming in waters my father could no longer reach.

I never saw children being killed. I never saw anyone killed. The war took place many miles from the kibbutz. In the cotton fields or chicken coops, the cow sheds or laundry room, every half hour we all stopped work and huddled around a transistor radio, listening to the latest war bulletin like teenage boys listening for the score of a baseball game.

Today, sitting at my white kitchen table, sipping a cup of Lapsang Souchong and listening to the November rain beat down on the roof of my house, I realize my life of adventure was founded on my father's dreams. The war I lived through at a distance in Israel was one he would have loved to fight. Instead of becoming the dutiful daughter and fulfilling the dreams he had for me, I realized the kind of life he could only imagine for himself. Instead of marrying someone from my own country and religion as he had, I married an Italian Catholic.

In my adventures, I found some of the missing pieces to the puzzle of that complex and unfulfilled man who was my father. Teatime, that sweet destination, a golden rim that shimmers on the surface of my memory, weaves my father and me together, fellow travelers on separate yet intricately entwined journeys. My father—a man old enough to be my grandfather, a man who died before I knew how to reconcile, a man whose dreams I inherited and fulfilled—will always have a seat at my table.

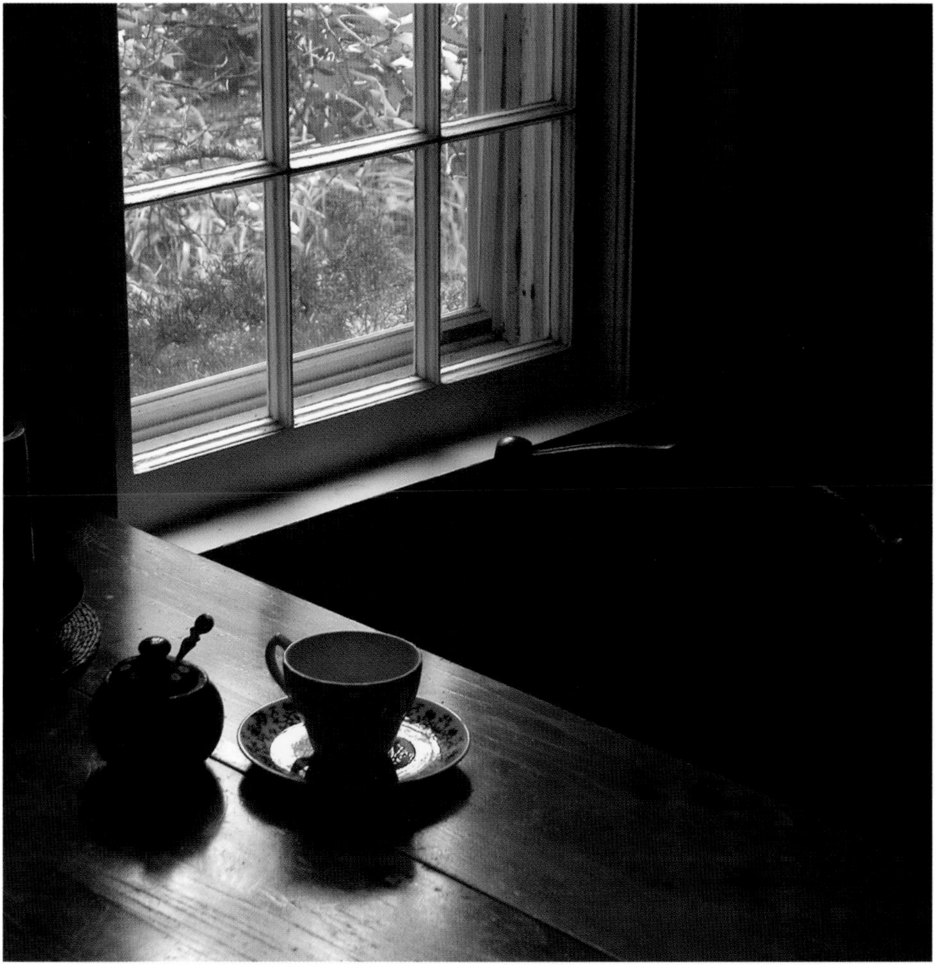

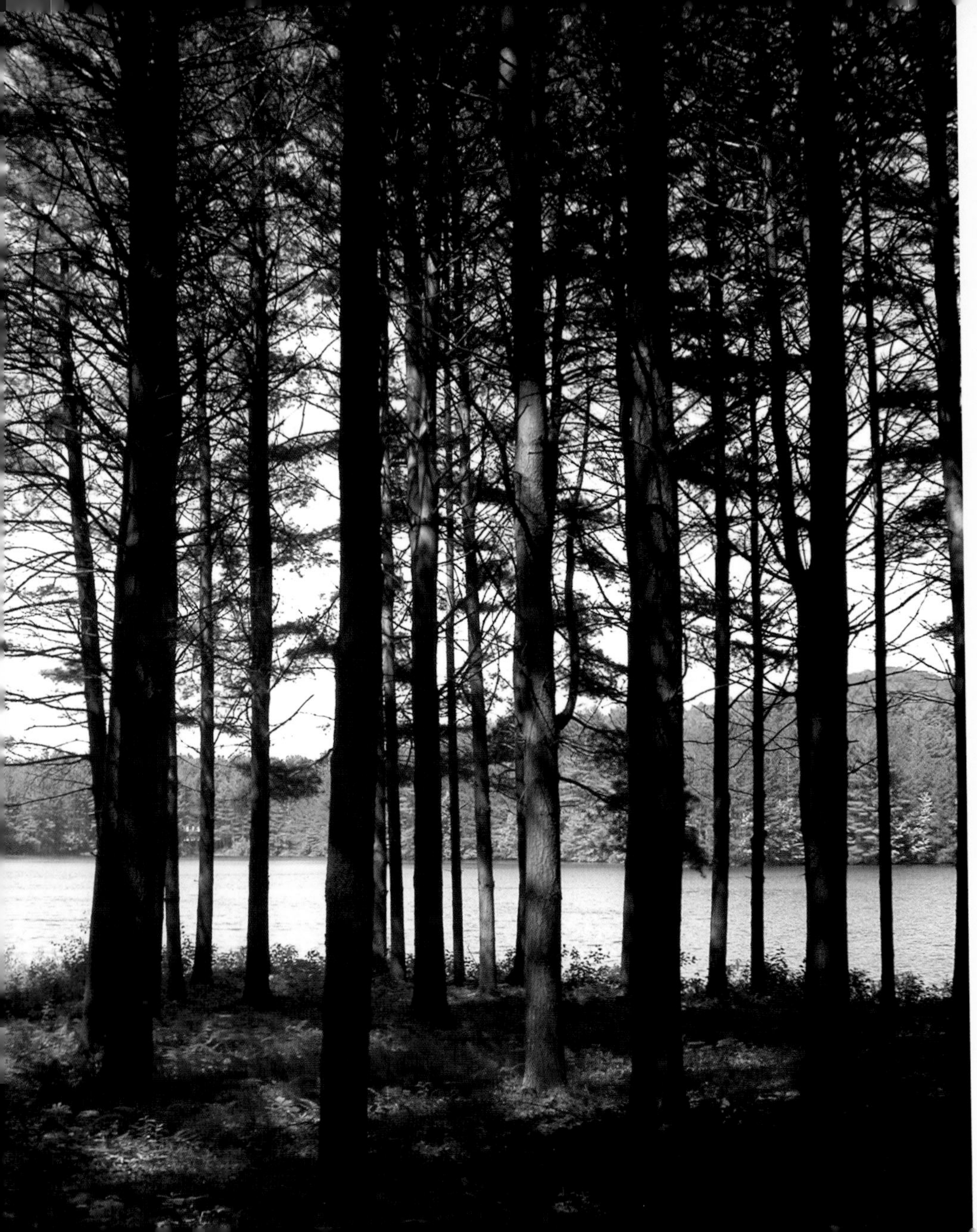

When Mom Was a Hippie

by Emily North

Living in Vermont in 1990, and convinced that civilization would soon be coming to an abrupt end, I moved with my daughter, Violet, from the small liberal arts college I had been attending, to a cabin on a dirt road. Armed with my cloth bound copy of *Indian Herbology of North America*, we gathered herbs to use as medicine and I taught myself how to use them.

My daughter was three that year and, squatting with her berry stained feet in pine needles, could explain the difference between true and false Solomon's seal. The difference? The leaves of the false Solomon's seal are larger. We gathered the roots of both, along with sarsaparilla, plantain, and raspberry leaves, to stock my kitchen; I wanted to be prepared for any illness that might strike us.

We set out each morning by seven to gather the herbs, down Moss Hollow Road, a dirt engraving through several hundred acres of virgin forest in Marlboro, Vermont. In the early light, the plants, wet with mercurial dew, glistened silver. Our search took us deep into woods so

vast we sometimes got lost until we found the stream that ran north of the cabin. In late spring, we stopped at a field where violets, her namesake, grew flush inside the rim of a bowl carved from tall grass. We filled our baskets for breakfast tea, purple with sunshiny dandelions.

Once, while gathering herbs for tea, Violet and I knelt in hushed solemnity over Indian pipe; Violet's towhead bent over the pages of the book before we learned its name. Indian pipe stands a few inches high, and glows translucent, mucilaginous smoking bows standing on end. Growing in clumps; magical, feathery, they wait for fairies to alight with opium.

In the afternoons, we sorted the herbs, shaking the dirt off and laying them along the counter. Violet helped me tie the roots into bunches to hang from the rafters, and we layered small leaves on baking sheets to dry in the sun. Sewing the thicker leaves into garlands, I zigzagged them across the ceiling. After the herbs and roots had dried, we trans-ferred them to bottles of all sizes and shapes. We had herbs for scant menstruation, stomach problems, allergies and flu. In addition, I stored juniper berries to prevent a miscarriage, tansy to bring one on, and of course, white willow bark for headaches.

For medicinal purposes, one either infuses or decocts the herb, depending on its properties and intended use. For an infusion, one steeps the herb or chopped root in boiling water for as little as ten minutes or as long as a day. When preparing raspberry leaves, most commonly used for pregnancy and lactation, one pours a pitcher of boiling water over the leaves to sit overnight before straining and drinking. For a decoction, the herbs are directly boiled in water for a certain amount of time. In either case, one needs to prepare the medicine in ceramic, not metallic containers, or risk losing valuable properties.

That summer, Violet asked for *The Poppy Seed Cakes* story every night. By the end of June, I had it memorized and recited it while thinking of shopping lists and laundry I needed to wash out in the tub that night. Violet was an easy child. Precocious, she carried on conversations with our cats, while they sat, attentive, appearing to listen. Our bedroom had a picture window, framing the evening's descent over the tops of pines as it settled into the nooks of the field surrounding the cabin. Dusk brought the coyotes passing by in the east. We paused during the story to listen to them.

With Violet in bed, I lit the candles in the kitchen and made a cup of tea; often yarrow, which resembles Queen Anne's lace and grows in meadows. Yarrow reminds me of August, just before the summer begins turning to fall, which it does in Vermont before September. If on one night in August there is a new crispness in the air, then by next morning, the spiders will have strewn the meadow and raspberry bushes with sodden webs. Thus, the smell of fall arrives, along with the golden rod, and this is how you know summer is passing.

At night, I sat on the front step to watch the stars while sipping my tea. Yarrow allegedly enhances psychic powers; the fields and woods around me thrummed with unexplained noises. On a stretch of the road a mile away, a ghost woman was said to approach cars on foggy nights. Believing the earth was on the verge of metamorphosis, I watched every evening for UFOs. My landlord, who lived in the other side of the house, joined me outside with his own cup of black tea.

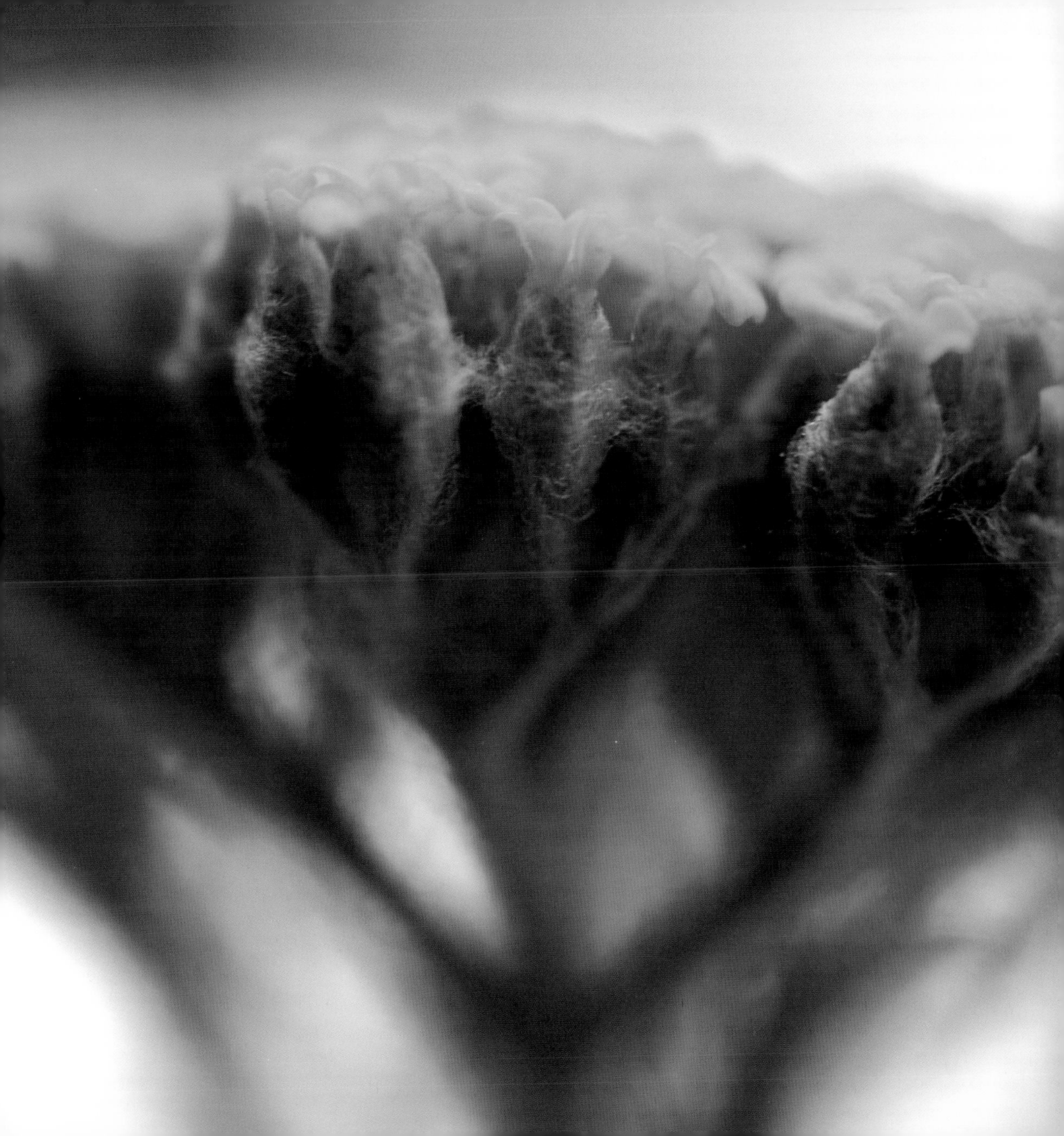

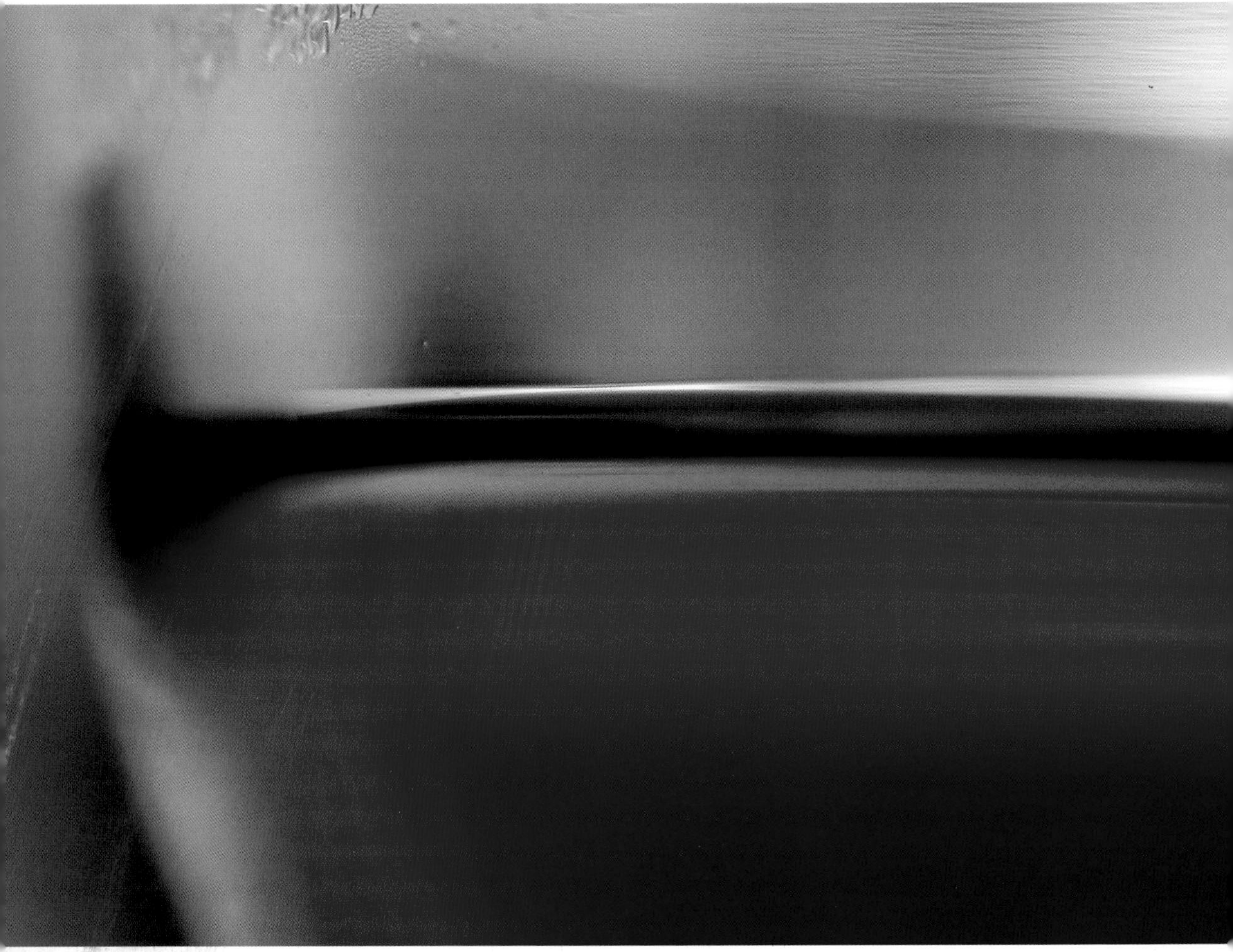

With a Ph.D. in Classics and dressed always in a white shirt and tie, he shared his belief that UFOs were humans in the future, returning to make contact with their past.

When the seasons kept passing, and the earth continually did not end, we moved out of the woods and rejoined the world. It is not so bad a place. I held onto herbal medicine until I became too busy with babies and graduate school.

Now that I have a real job and health insurance, it is easier to simply take the kids to the doctor. Violet has turned fourteen and looks back at our past as the days when "My mom was a hippie," which she says with a mix of incredulity and scorn.

Violet and I still garden together. Leaving her brothers with a sitter, we roam back roads together in our battered Volvo, seeking farm stands with hanging plants, heirloom hollyhocks, and vivid delphiniums. I do not watch the stars every night anymore, but if I can think of it, and if I can coax Violet from the TV, we sit on the porch steps in the dark. Warming our hands around cups of tea, we look into the sky and wonder.

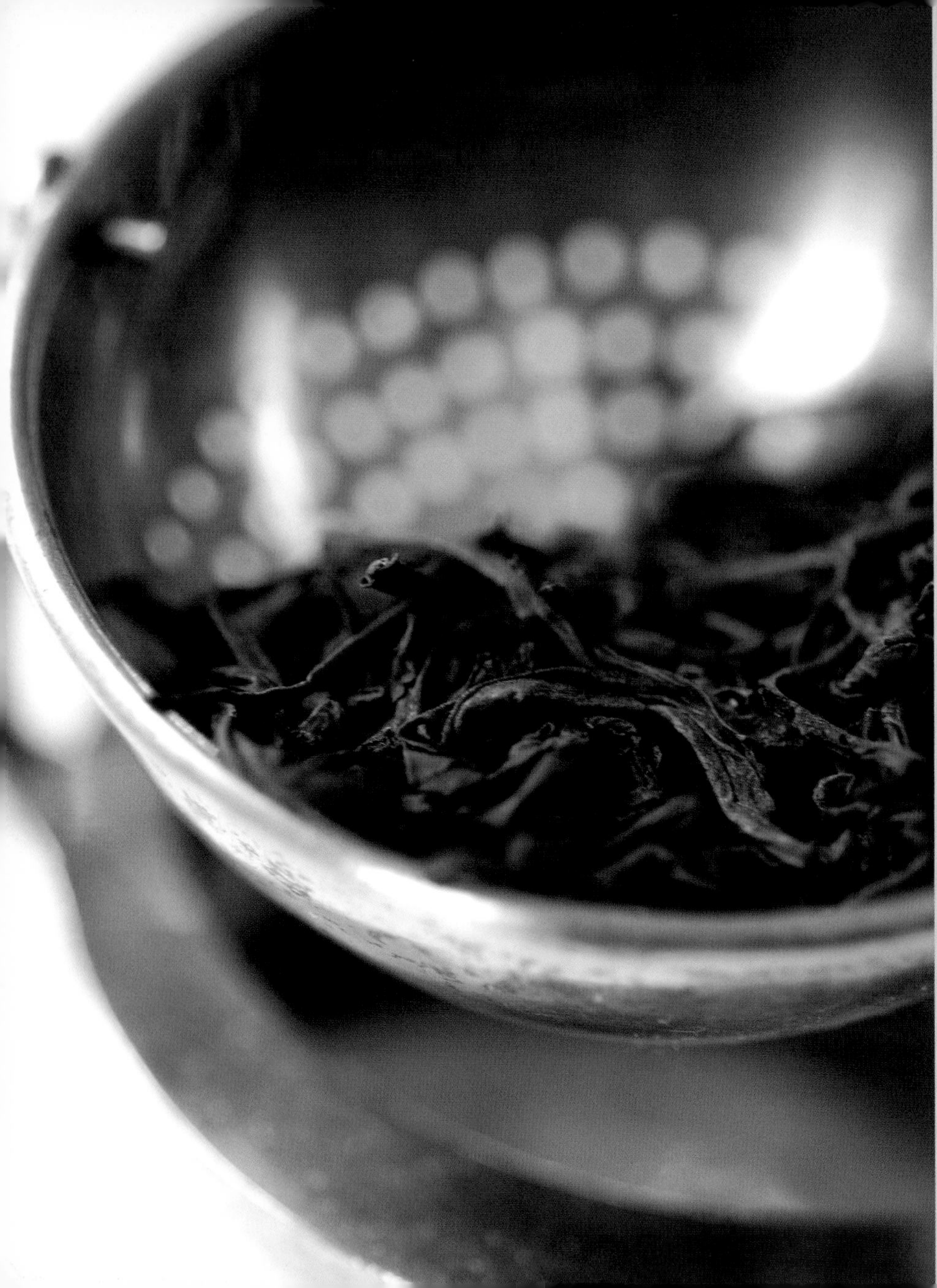

CLOSED EYES SMILING

By D.L. DuBois

It was a chilly morning; the mist had not yet retracted its gray embrace from the rows and rows of stout tea plants terracing the hills. It sent a chill up her spine. She gathered the pashmina shawl around her and took another sip, remembering the fine golden drape the Tibetan painter had worn. Surely this liquid gold would be of the same nature as his cloth if it were captured in weft and weave.

He had shown her his latest work, a White Tara sitting in the lotus position with a mystic eye in her upturned feet, her meditation-poised palms, her forehead. He carefully painted the Tara's gold anklet with a fine hair brush as she looked on.

"You like it?" he asked smiling with teeth like an uneven whitewashed fence.

"Very much," Maeli replied. "It is lovely."

"What do you like?"

"The calmness, I suppose. She seems content."

The old man furrowed his leathery brow in confusion.

"She seems happy."

"Yes, yes, happy. She is Goddess of prosperity and wisdom. She protects the house."

"Could I buy it?" Maeli said, knowing she had just given up her right to barter. A foreigner requesting an object with obvious interest gave the vendor full rights to inflate the price.

"Not for sale. I make it for a temple. Festival of Buddha is coming soon."

"Do you have another one?"

"Only drawings. No painting," the old man said stopping to lift the delicate hairs from the last golden bead on the anklet.

"Well, it is beautiful. It makes me feel happy to look at it."

"You are not happy?"

"Yes, well, sort of. As much as anybody, I guess."

"That is sad," the old painter said as he carefully washed the paint from the delicate brush. "No one in the West is happy. Money is god there. Lord Buddha left his wealth to find peace."

"Money is not all bad," Maeli said in a drifting voice. "It buys food, clothes, shoes. You need those things too."

The old man motioned for her to sit on the stool beside him.

"Yes. I paint for those things. In Tibet I was temple painter. I lived in small room with other monks, rolled up my cotton bed and put in corner before morning meditation, painted walls and hanging scrolls, mandalas and Buddhas. I painted for prayer. Now I paint for food, clothes, and shoes, a refugee in this center the Americans gave us. I paint for tourists."

"But this Tara, it is not for tourists."

"It is for a temple in America. Much money comes from orders from temples there, and shops," he said with evident sadness.

"It is still for prayer."

"It is. Lord Buddha has great compassion. We are cast out of our home to learn new life, but we survive. We share Lord Buddha with the West."

A loud bell rang making Maeli jump.

"What is that?"

"Tea time. We go to canteen for tea, all the workers."

"Well, I guess I'd better go now. Thank you for showing me your painting. It is beautiful and peaceful."

"You want tea? I fix it here for you," he said pointing to a small clay-lined metal pot on the wooden ledge next to his jars of paint.

"I don't want to bother you."

"Do you want to join me?" he said, tilting his head back a bit to better see from under his droopy lids.

"Yes, thank you."

"I make better tea than canteen. They drink with milk and sugar and boil the tea too long."

The old man carefully put his cleaned brush on a rest and rose slowly from his stool. At full height he came to Maeli's shoulder. Carefully he blew into the small hole at the bottom of the metal pot to activate the sleeping embers. A curl of blue smoke rose up and drifted towards the ceiling. He opened a can and lifted a small paper-wrapped packet of tea and scooped some leaves into his cupped hands. He blew over them gently to warm them. Taking a deep breath of the dark, curled leaves he smiled.

"From here, finest second growth, picked before the monsoons. My nephew works at a tea estate. He gave me."

He held the leaves up to Maeli's nose. She took in the earthy aroma.

"From Kalimpong area, to east. As boy I walked with father to Kalimpong to sell tea." His mouth turned down, pursing tightly over

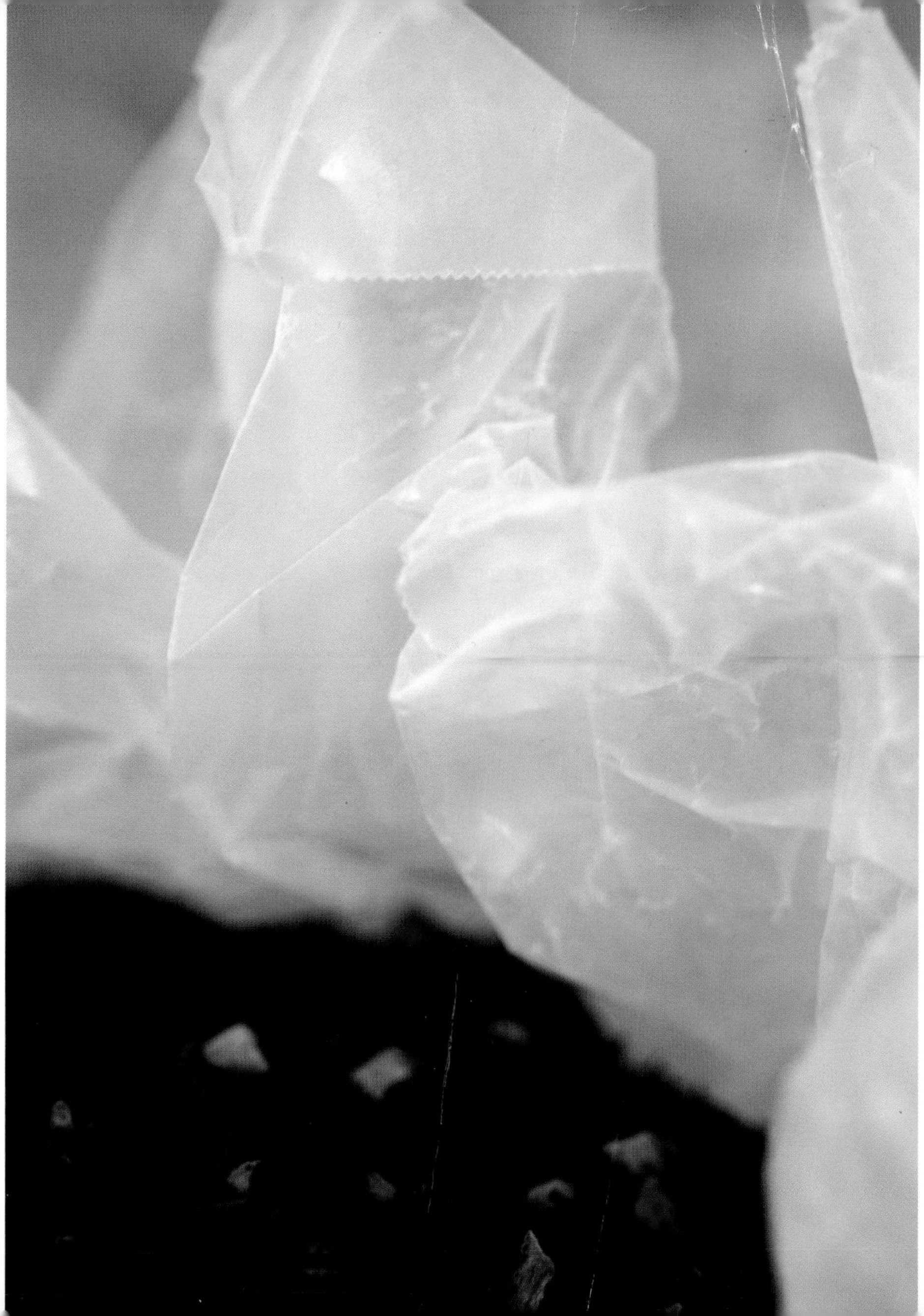

his uneven teeth. "That was when we were free… before China invaded. Now we live here in camp. Chinese hate Tibetans, want them to be Chinese servants."

Maeli winced at her ancestry and changed the subject to the making of tea.

"How do you make your tea?"

"Boil water, good boil," he said as he filled the pot from a nearby pitcher of water, "but never boil the leaves. Bitter tea is a waste of life." The old man padded in his slippers to the other side of the small cabin and lifted a piece of board to reveal sheets of drawings. He motioned for Maeli to come look.

"Buddha in meditation."

He held up one diagrammatic drawing after another showing Lord Buddha in various meditation poses.

"I will paint these."

"You draw them first, always?"

"Yes, yes. My father sent me to school to learn this. Teacher made us draw, copy his sketches. He learned from master teacher. I work in his tradition."

"Each one is the same as his?"

"Each one, just the same. Only master artist monk could make change in drawing. Students must follow exactly. Lord Buddha gives master artist monk way to see and others follow. I follow."

The bubbling water spilled over onto the coals and sizzled. The old man shuffled back to the bench. Pulling a small spoon from a cloth sheath, he measured three level spoonfuls into a glass dish. Removing the metal teapot with a mitt, he poured a little boiling water into a porcelain pot and rinsed it before carefully dropping in the curled tea leaves. He glanced at a watch face lying like a solitary eye on his painting table.

"Exact three minutes. No more. No less."

Maeli continued studying the diagrams, geometric grids overlayed with a Buddha seated on a lotus throne, each sketch varying in hand positions, while the old man set out two small porcelain cups at his painting table. Gently he wrapped the teapot in a cloth and shuffled over to pour Maeli and himself tea.

The golden liquid seemed to glow in the dingy room. He wrapped his hands completely around his cup holding it close to savor a long, deliberate sip. He closed his eyes and drifted to his childhood when he and his father would stop on their trek and take tea with the merchants who plied the path over the mountains to Kalimpong. He felt his father's jacket brush his face as the pack horse, weighed down with woven baskets full of tea leaves, gingerly picked its way along the narrow mountain trail. He recalled his father's scent, a mixture of wood smoke, fermented tea leaves, and leather.

He opened his tired lids and looked at Maeli. "The Chinese killed my father in the invasion. He said Lord Buddha wanted him to fight. He left me in charge of my mother and sister and went to fight. I was nineteen. My mother said Lord Buddha would protect him. Two months later winter set in. He never came home. The next spring a man came to tell us father was dead. I knew we had to leave. I led us over the mountains to India. Our feet bled from the rocks. We wrapped them in cloth and kept walking. Snowfields slowed us. We kept walking. Hunger made us weak. We kept walking. When we reached Darjeeling we were starving. Mother died two days after we crossed border. Now I sit here with other refugees and paint for my food and shelter. I am lucky. My sister weaves on the loom. She is lucky. Many died. Lord Buddha is full of compassion."

Maeli looked down into her cup of tea and pressed back the moisture collecting in her eyes realizing the painter was weathered from life, not years. She took a sip and recalled her father's story of his

father's flight in 1949 with Chiang Kai-shek to Taiwan and how his forebear had come by ship to California to lay railroad iron for the transcontinental railway before returning to China to marry. She decided not to share her family story.

"Well, you're lucky then."

"Death is not bad. It is a beginning. Suffering is a test to remember Lord Buddha."

"Are you suffering?" Maeli asked the old man who seemed to retreat to a distant place as he took a noisy slurp of tea.

"No more than you."

Maeli straightened up. "I am not suffering, Sir."

"You don't know. You can't see. Your eyes are closed."

Maeli felt slightly insulted but assumed the old man was not attacking her.

"I do see."

"What?"

"Well, I see the world as it is. I see the tea in this cup."

"Do you see the hand that picked it?"

"No."

"Do you see the heavy basket on the woman's back? Do you see her baby strapped to her chest? Do you see her aching feet as she walks the hills?"

"No."

"Then you don't see. Take a sip. Close your eyes."

Maeli took a warm sip and smelled the pungent aroma. She felt the cool mist on her skin. She saw her hand reach down to the bush and pluck the top three leaves from each stem. Deftly she gathered until both hands bulged with glossy leaves and she tossed them over her head into the basket. She wound her way along the terraced hill back and forth, picking until her basket made it difficult for her to stand upright. She felt her sandaled feet ache from the weight of the tea and the infant sleeping at her chest. When she opened her eyes, the heaviness left her limbs.

"That was strange. It was like I really was there, in what you said."

"That was concentration. The tea has given you a gift. Use it."

"What gift?"

"The gift of compassion. You felt what I said. You understood. Now I will paint for you a White Tara. Now you will understand. It is as Lord Buddha wants, to look upon it and understand."

Maeli took her last sip of tea and looked at the weathered face of the painter. He pulled a sketch from under the board and placed it on his table.

"I don't paint for tourists,' he said, "I paint for prayer."

Maeli looked at the Tibetan and saw the setting sun, the amber color of Darjeeling tea, in his eyes.

"Sir, I feel I must say something to you before you make such a gift for me."

"Yes?"

"I am half Chinese. My father is Chinese."

"And your father's father?"

"Yes, he is Chinese."

"I know. I saw it in your eyes. They are much like mine."

Maeli looked down at the tiny leaf floating in the well of her cup. When she raised her eyes, the old man's met hers.

"With this tea you taste the heart of our mountains," he said and enjoyed a sip with closed eyes smiling.

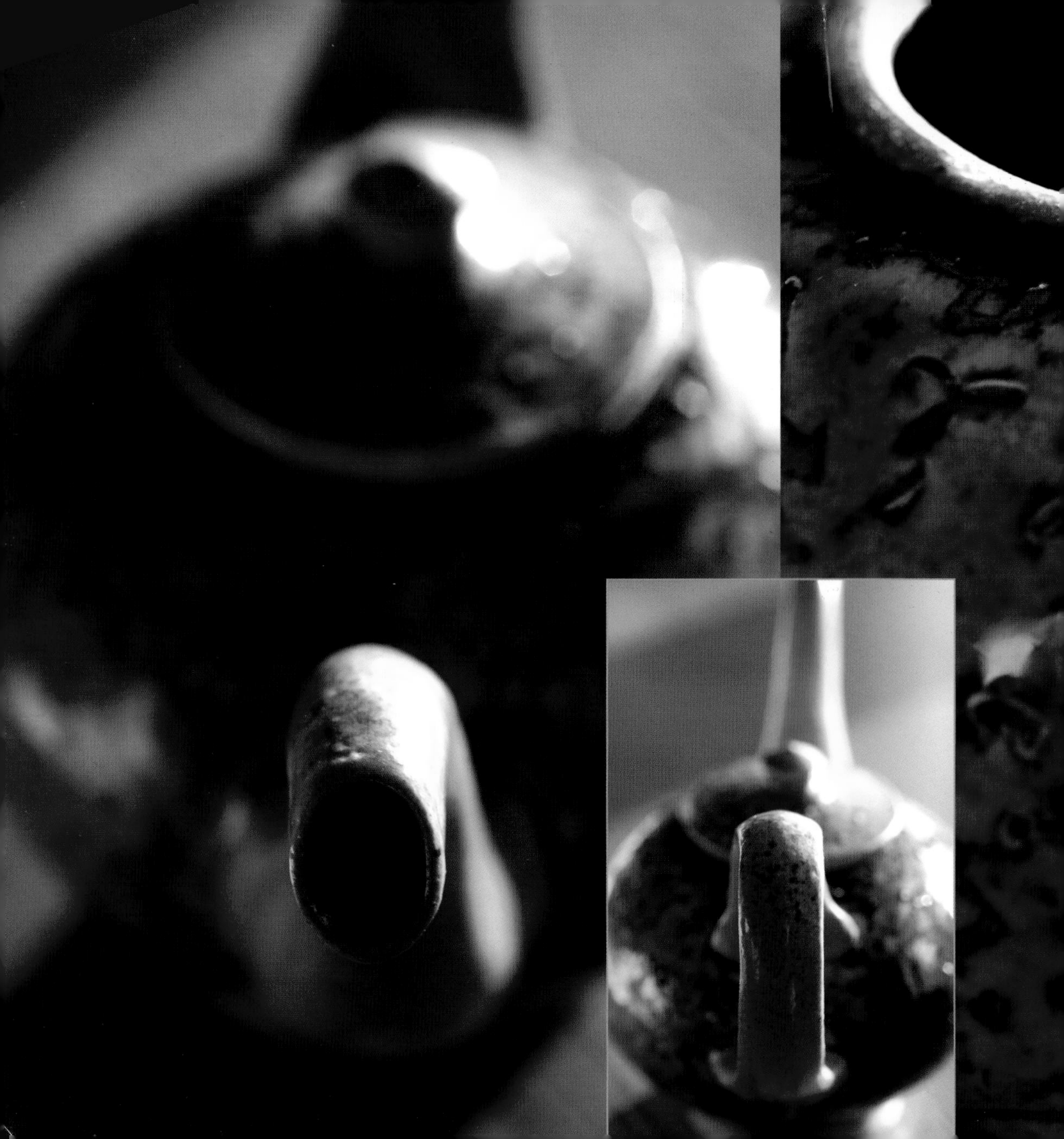

PASSAGE

by M. Romo-Carmona

2000— The year began with the opening of a red tin, tightly sealed with its golden lid. I dropped a fingerful of leaves in the small Japanese teapot when the water boiled, then stood beside it for a moment to catch the first rising of steamy aroma before covering the pot.

1992— Before I could sit down to write I had to organize all our dishes. I moved the cups from one cabinet to the other, all the pretty ones together. My lover cannot appreciate my logic. And she prefers coffee.

1987— But I remember she never cared what her cup looked like, a yellow mug or a blue one, or the small cup with the apples. This year, she asked for her favorite.

1960— In downtown Santiago, the café Paula was my palace. My mother took me there on special occasions to have a slice of cake with chantilly cream. When I went back thirty years later, it was only a modest coffee shop. One has to be eight years old to see the palace.

1957— Every time there was an earth tremor, we ran to stand under the half-open doorway for protection. Only the cement wall outside developed a thin crack after many, many years. On the shelf, the two pretty teacups shook and clinked, but never fell down.

1959— At my grandmother's house, she drank *maté* in a round cup made just for *maté*, round like a calabash. She put sugar in it, that she toasted on the coal fire, and she sipped it through a silver straw.

1958— I must have been very little when I got my own *maté* cup, and a silver sipping straw from Argentina. The sipper is the length of a pencil, with a perforated ball at one end. You sip the tea when it's hot, making satisfying pulls with your lips.

2001— There's something of the witch in me, in winter.

1999— Before our kitchen was blue it had no color. I made tea and smelled my lover's neck as she bent over her cup. Her hair fell back again, heavy with gloss.

1986— San Francisco was so cold the first time we went there. I look at the small white pot with pale blue hydrangea that we bought; it has matching cups. Two round, two cylindrical. Our friend, Pauline, explained that the taller cups are given to the men, so they will not burn their fingers.

1998— I realized that I hadn't had tea in ages. My favorite cup this year is Japanese. It reads, "If you fall down seven times, you get up eight times."

1998— Last year I strayed. Tins of tea sat like soldiers in the back reaches of the cabinets while I flirted with coffee.

1981— With the blue ink from my fountain pen I want to write an incantation; with this brew I'll make a wish.

1978— In the middle of a snow storm there's a coffee shop that's open. Somewhere my old girlfriend is calling her new girlfriend. Everything clinks and clatters inside the coffee shop. The waitress brings me tea in a chipped cup and the water is very, very hot. The windows of the shop steam up against the snow.

1997— Venturing into jasmine tea my tongue resists the flavor. I will try again another year.

1990— Once, my mother gave me a box of gunpowder tea. It is green tea, the leaves rolled up tightly into pellets. The tiny balls unfurl in the pot. My mother tells me I have not changed.

1995— Mango tea comes in a rectangular red tin. Spice and vanilla tea come in oval tins, painted black, with pink flowers. Green tea must be served as soon as one brings the water to the pot. And I have lychee, persimmon, and passionfruit. Too many varieties, like my unfinished stories.

1993— The year my son came to visit I remembered he didn't drink anything hot. Not even coffee. But when he was a child he liked herbal tea with honey, and he asked me for that again. I saw that what we shared was not what I expected.

1975— I'm looking for someone to read my fortune.

1996— Milyoung came to visit us one day, and she brought us Korean corn and barley tea. We all had some after dinner; it is good for the digestion. I made it in the old blue earthenware pot.

1988— When our cat is sick, she wakes up with sticky stuff around her eyelids. I use a teabag to make a strong cup and put it aside. When it cools I hold Cleo wrapped in a towel, and I wash her eyes with tea and a cotton ball. Cleo walks away shaking her fur, trying to be dignified.

1997— My cousin comes from Chile to see us in New York. We talk for days; nights, too. She shows me the way my mother taught her mother to make tea 45 years ago. My mother says she never made tea like that.

1994— My mother and I are happy shopping in Chinatown. I've bought the most delicious oolong.

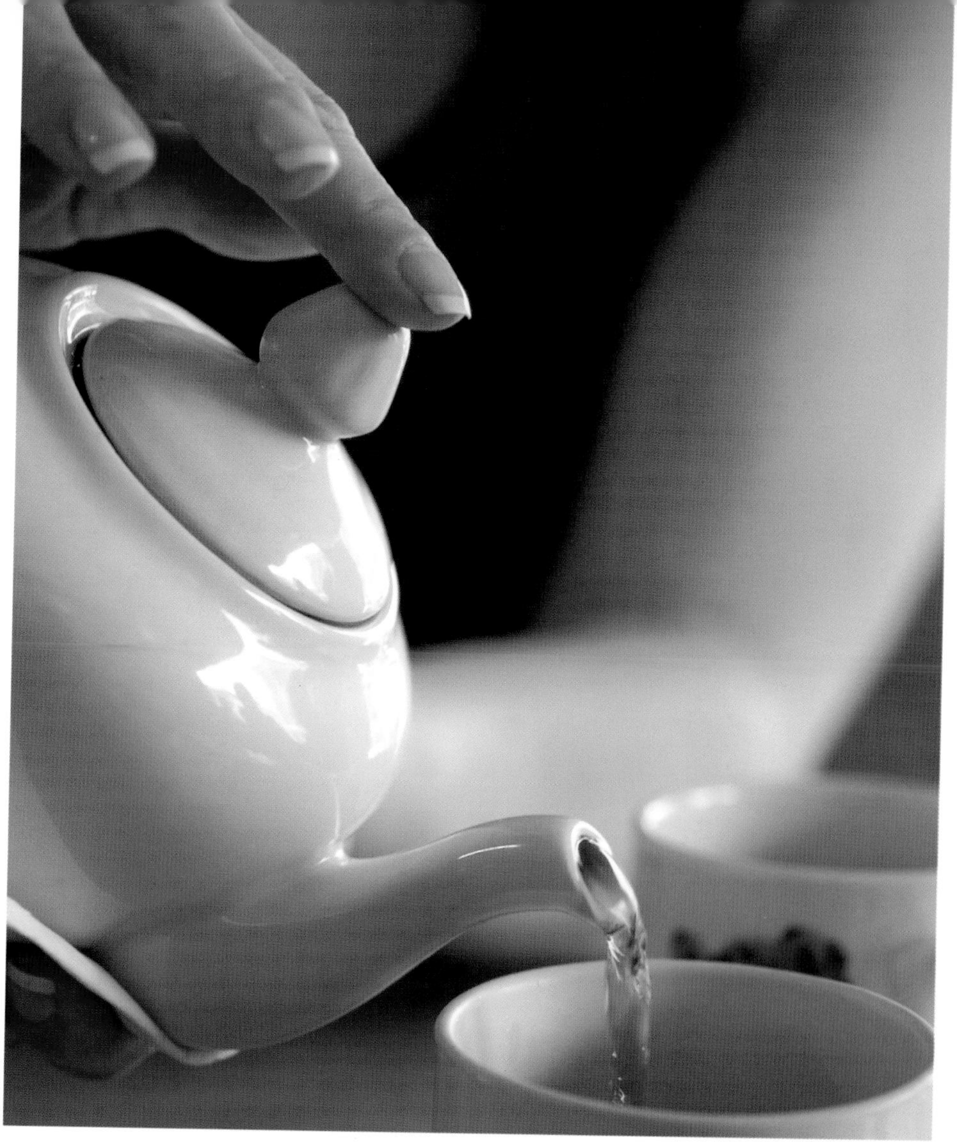

1978— It was a white mug, smooth glaze inside and out. A teddy bear with a red ribbon sits inside it. My son is four and he likes to drink cool Pelican tea with honey from his cup, squealing with delight when he sees the bear's head above the liquid. Should I have gotten him the cup? One day he drowns gummy bears in the tea.

1957— When I was five I knew that one must not slurp tea from the spoon or from the cup. I'm amazed when I see our visitor do it, an important guest. My mother looks at me. I know I should not laugh, but I smile.

1957— The other rule is that even when drinking hot *té con leche*, I must not ask for it to be poured in the saucer for me, to cool. Grandmother does it for me anyway. My mother knows I'm spoiled.

1962— Only when the water boils can the tea be prepared. I wait, impatient. If I pour it into the pot before it boils, it will be foamy in the cup. I try it anyway. It's an experiment. There's a tiny bubble remaining in the amber whirlpool, and I remove it. I carry it slowly, in the very best cup. My mother looks at me. How did she know?

1960— *Té. Un té. ¿qué te sirvo?* Un té no más. Inflections vary. Grandfather died. My mother wears black. She still makes the tea.

1961— *¿Un tesito?* A little tea, a diminutive tea. That means affection. A friend who visits. It could be you have a cold. It could be there's not much time for a long tea.

1963— *Ven a tomar el té.* That means "onces," the meal we have at five. *El té* means bread, too, and blackberry jam, quince preserves, pastry or ham and cheese and avocado. When there's no money for any of this, life is the same. There's tea.

1964— But if you say *ven a tomar té*, that means any tea, at any time. Just come and visit, and you might not even drink tea that day, you'll have *charquicán*. Chileans speak in riddles.

1979— Summer in Connecticut. After the beach my roommate and I bought a blue pot. Handmade pottery, round, perfect shape, thin spout that doesn't drip outside the cup. The blue glaze has a little green in it, and a touch of brown. When I close my eyes I see the ocean.

1983— She invites me to have sushi in New York, my first time. I enjoyed the dishes just as much as the food. I traced the plum blossoms on the tea cup over and over with my fingers, wanting to memorize their simplicity. My new love watches me, bemused.

1984— When I moved that year, I gave my roommate $7.50 for her share of the blue pot, so I could take it with me to New York. When I close my eyes I see I am still young.

1959— I carry the perfect cup of tea for my mother, teaspoon in the saucer, no little fountains spilling over. I walk slowly over the red tiles.

1983— My lover takes me home to meet her mother. Her tea steeps in a covered white mug with a blue dragon, and she offers me half her orange.

1967— It's the immigrant 60s; the winter is seven months long. A boy brought my mother a cup of tea at an ice cream parlor in Connecticut. No one spoke Spanish except us. The cup was two inches thick with a red stripe around it, the edge was chipped, the water was cold, the tea bag floated yellow, still half dry. I put a dime in the juke-box and listened to the Supremes.

1956— One was pale pink, with raised black and golden designs of a dragon around the cup and the saucer. The other cup had chrysanthemums, red and yellow on a black background. The porcelain was so thin, I could almost see through it. They were a present to my mother from tío Julio, who also loved beautiful things.

1984— When I moved to New York, I walked into a shop on Canal Street; it was better than Tiffany's. You can sample the most fragrant teas in diminutive terra cotta cups, and choose the one that will bring the ritual back again, all the aroma, the flavor, the perfect color.

2002— And one day I remembered the blue tin with the gold fish and golden edges at the back of the cabinet. I'm looking for a way not to forget.

1965— The red tiles have been waxed and buffed until they shine. I walk on them with my white summer shoes, being careful not to spill the orange pekoe in the cup.

2002— The fountain pen I love leaks and stains my fingers. Writing this story, I had to change some of the dates.

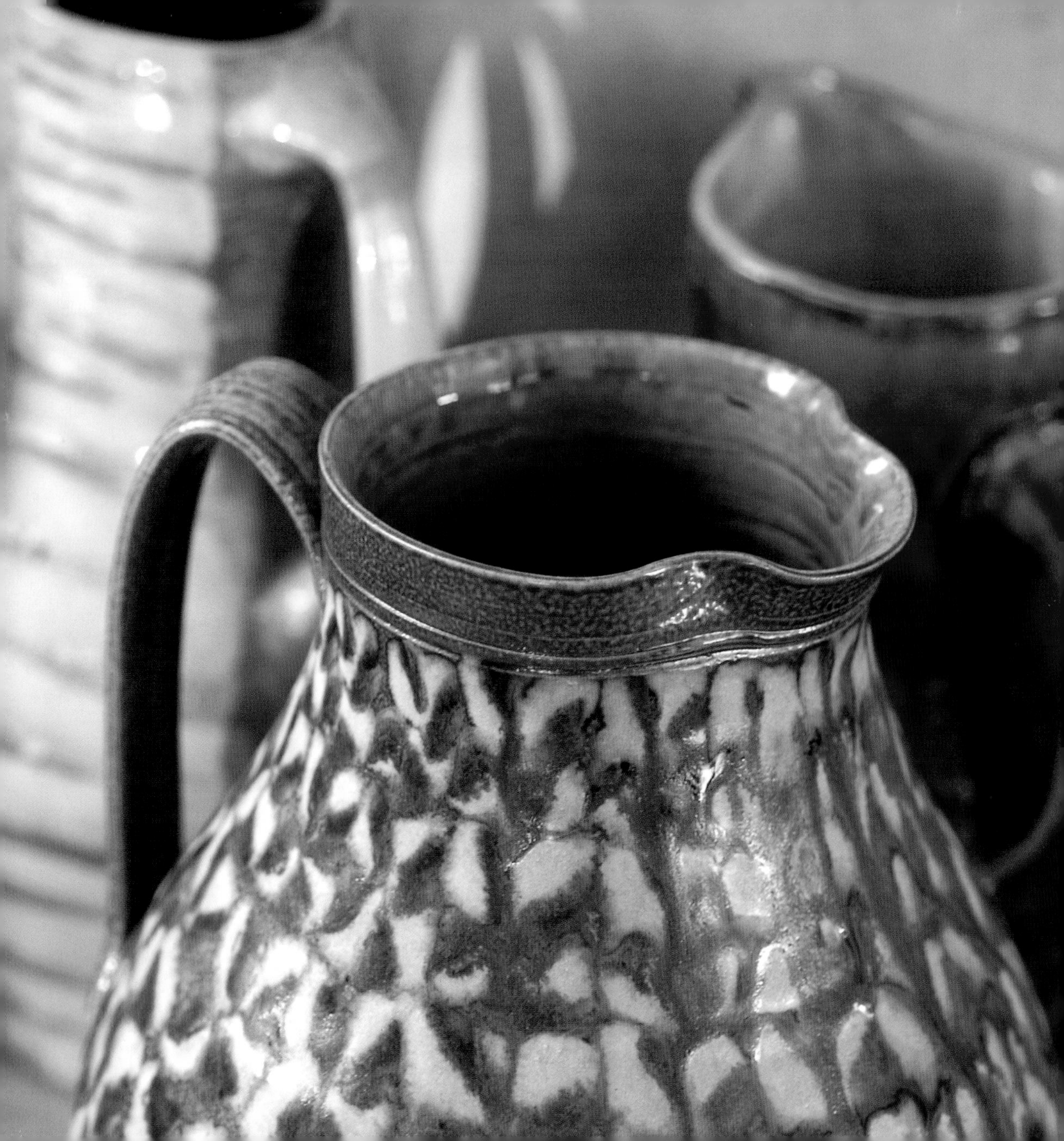

C'EST BON, ÇA...

by Meredith Escudier

I grew up in fifties America in a family that regarded beverages with a prescription-for-what-ails-you philosophy. Frothy milkshakes soothed sore throats and tonsillectomies. Orange juice buttressed defenses against colds. Water could ward off most anything. We even had a pediatrician whose recommendation for a nasty bout of mumps was Coca Cola, a panacea later considered exotic and outrageously American by the French friends with whom I spent the next portion of my life. The beverage that endured, however, was tea. Hot tea. It made its appearance in my early life as antidote of choice for the fragile, weakened, and woozy state of an upset stomach. It had a settling effect, I was told, and it did. I snuggled cozily in my bed, comforted by a tray of tea and toast on the one hand and a selection of Archie Comics on the other. With a renewed sense of self-importance, I took careful, calculated sips. My childish taste buds were not yet up to appreciation of the beverage, but I had assimilated one important lesson: tea had healing properties.

In the sixties, when I spent my first year in France in the southwest, tea started to edge its way into a ritual for me. For natives of this region, five o'clock ladies' tea was a link with the English, through Eleanor of Aquitaine. Eleanor was first the wife of Henry VII of France and later married Henry II of England. Tea was thus royal, a tribute to a page of history only eight centuries away.

My French mother-in-law made it in a little earthenware teapot. Teabags. Chipped cups with broken handles. Packaged cookies. We didn't mind. It was a woman's moment and I felt refined, sipping tea with sugar, speculating about the weather in French, harking back to Eleanor.

An English friend introduced me to loose tea from Harrod's, extracting spoonfuls from a little blue paper pouch with her silver spoon. Both young mothers, we visited each other once a week. To our four bouncing little boys we served one part tea to four or five parts milk. Our young tea drinkers stood on their chairs, crawled under the table, needed help wiping their noses, pounded on the walls for attention, and wailed if the biscuits were broken, bless their little hearts. We adults sat there in our sensible denim overalls and our motherly calm and sipped our tea as if we were in London's Fortnum and Mason tea salon, selecting dainties from a silver tray.

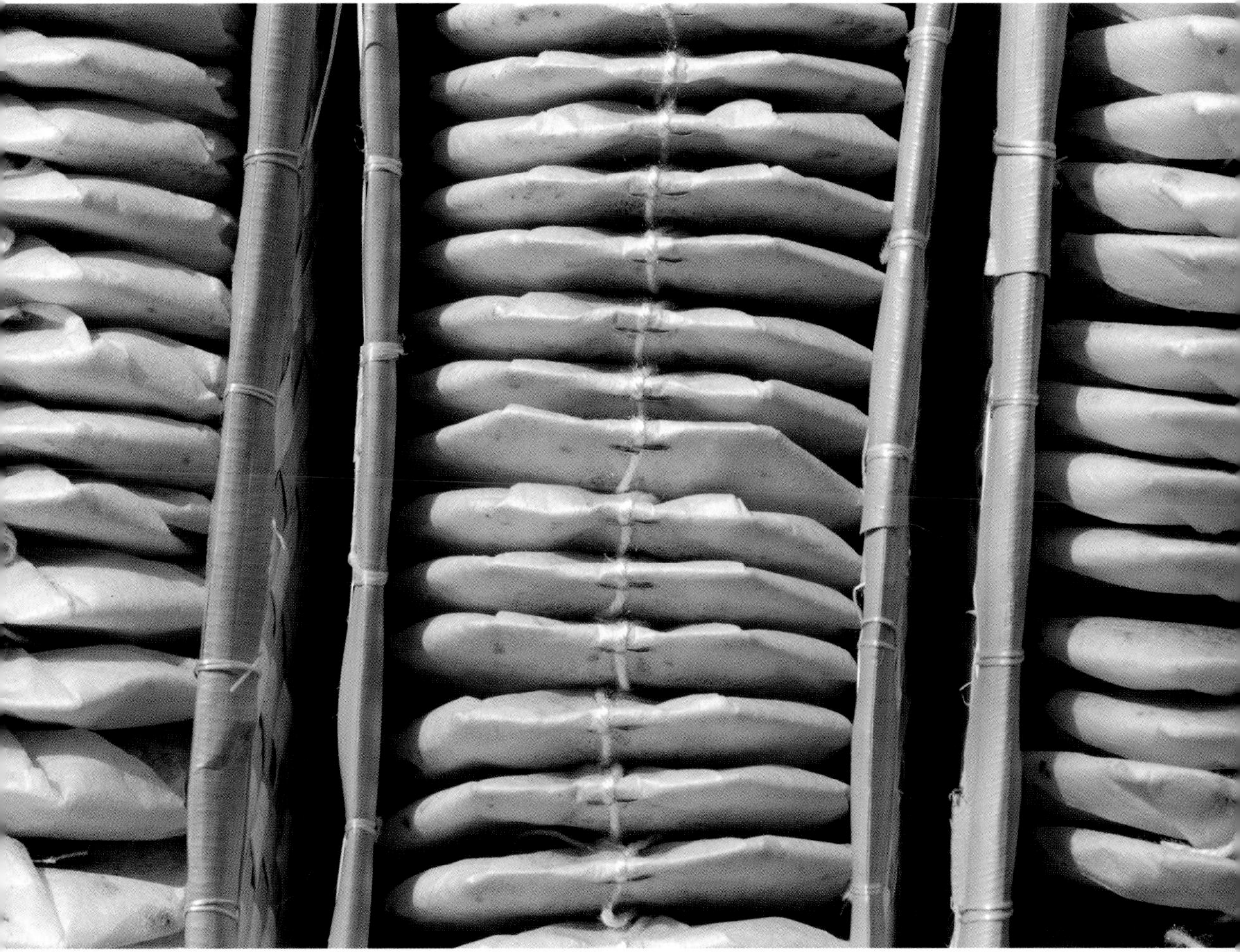

We invited a friend once, an English girl who arrived with a present for the little boys, saying "I brought their tea," as she handed it over to me.

"Their tea?" I looked down at the jam tartelettes wrapped in wax paper, then up again at her unperturbed face. So tea was not just a beverage or a time, it was also the solid stuff that went with it. The other part, the actual tea part, was taken for granted.

"Oh yes, of course, " I nodded. "Their tea."

My husband always went for a rough hunk of cheese and a torn baguette with his tea. I sampled it. *C'est bon, ça...* and a whole world of tea and savory opened up to me. Tea with camembert. Tea with ham, tea with quiche, tea with pita bread. Even high tea: cucumber sandwiches, canapés with smoked salmon, pâté, tarama, goat cheese.

It could be argued that love of tea is a road towards refinement, one that starts with a Lipton teabag and proceeds to a Japanese tea ceremony or an afternoon tea with the Queen, just as a wine connoisseur or a fine gourmet advances in sophistication and never looks back.

Tea is different, though. My family was right that tea's good for the body, but it heals the soul as well. It's time for the self. Tea is a conscious moment in time. Tea is what you make it. It can punctuate life with a chance moment of high harmony. That is why one of my

favorite tea memories is set in an air-conditioned Florida Dunkin'
Donuts, mid-morning.

Only ten A.M. and already the shimmering air outside announces the
scorcher to come. I sit at the counter with a steaming thick white mug
and watch the waitress in her crepe soles flirt with two tattooed cops, in
for their daily donuts and coffee. My Haitian friend is sitting next to me,
wearing a green sundress. We chat in French about her immigration
status. I fiddle with the napkin dispenser. I swirl the teabag around for a
few turns, remove it, and add a drop of non-dairy creamer. I lift my mug
to my lips and sip in its warmth in short little takes. Through the steam
I can see the waitress heft the coffee pot off the burner where it's been
simmering for hours, and give those cops the refill they've come to know
and love. I see only kindness, simplicity, humanity. All is at peace in the
world. She approaches me, her coffee pot not quite emptied.

"How's the coffee situation here?" She is cheerful, expectant,
ready to pour.

"Oh, I'm fine," I reassure her. "I'm having tea actually. Thanks."

"Okay, hon."

We smile at each other and she's off for another round. As she
turns, I notice how the bow of her apron is starched and neatly tied.

133

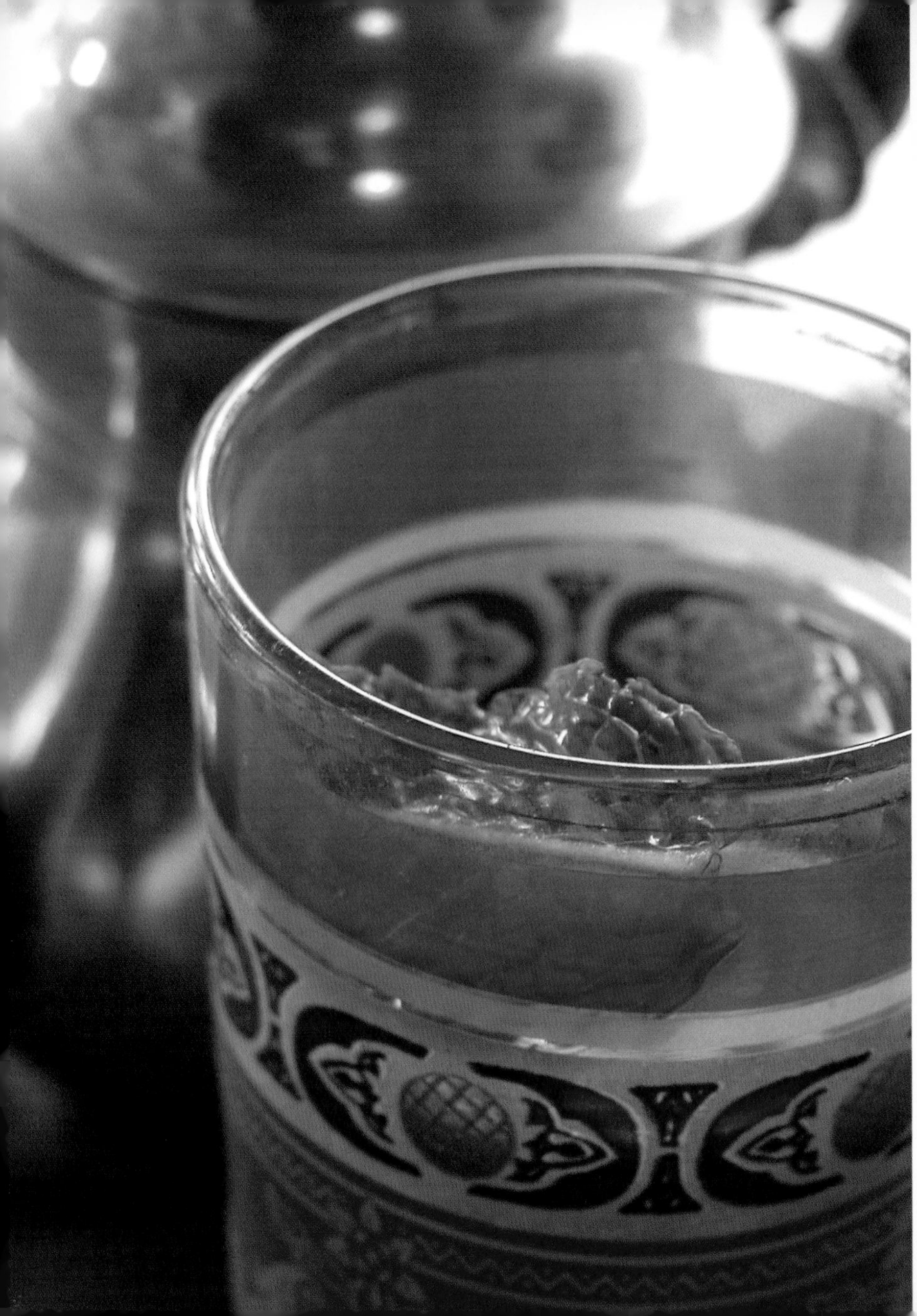

Moroccan Mint Tea

by Habeeb Salloum

The preparation and serving of *atay*, Morocco's most popular drink, is always offered in a ceremonial fashion. The person serving the tea usually brews it in front of the guests. In the process the server tastes the tea to make sure that it is ready, and then, holding the pot about two feet above, pours the tea into small decorated glasses. Usually dressed in colorful Moroccan costume, the server pours the tea in a string-like arc, never missing the glass. Pouring Moroccan tea is an acquired art—a truly picturesque scene in an exotic Moroccan setting.

This tea is drunk at all times of the day by Moroccans in every stratum of society. Whether served in a humble café, an elaborate restaurant, or in the home, this drink is the refreshment most loved by Moroccans and the other peoples of North Africa.

4 ½ cups boiling water

1 ½ tablespoons green tea
(if not available, Indian tea may be substituted)

½ cup of pressed fresh mint leaves with stalks
(dried mint leaves are not as good, but they can be used if
fresh mint is not available—use 2 teaspoons of finely
crushed mint leaves)

5 teaspoons of sugar

Rinse out a teapot with hot water; then add the tea. Pour in
½ cup of boiling water; then, to remove bitterness, swish the
tea and water around in the pot quickly. Discard the water,
but not the tea. Stuff the mint leaves with their stalks into
the pot, then add sugar and the remaining boiling water.
Allow to steep for 5 minutes, checking occasionally to make
sure the mint does not rise above the water. Stir and taste,
adding more sugar as needed before serving. *Serves 4.*

Note: For second helpings, leave the mint and tea in the pot and add another teaspoon of tea, several fresh mint leaves, and more sugar. Add again the same amount of boiling water. When the mint rises to the surface, the tea is ready. Stir and taste for sweetness; then serve. The same process can be repeated for the third pot. Also, the tea can be served without sugar, so guests can add sugar to suit their own taste.

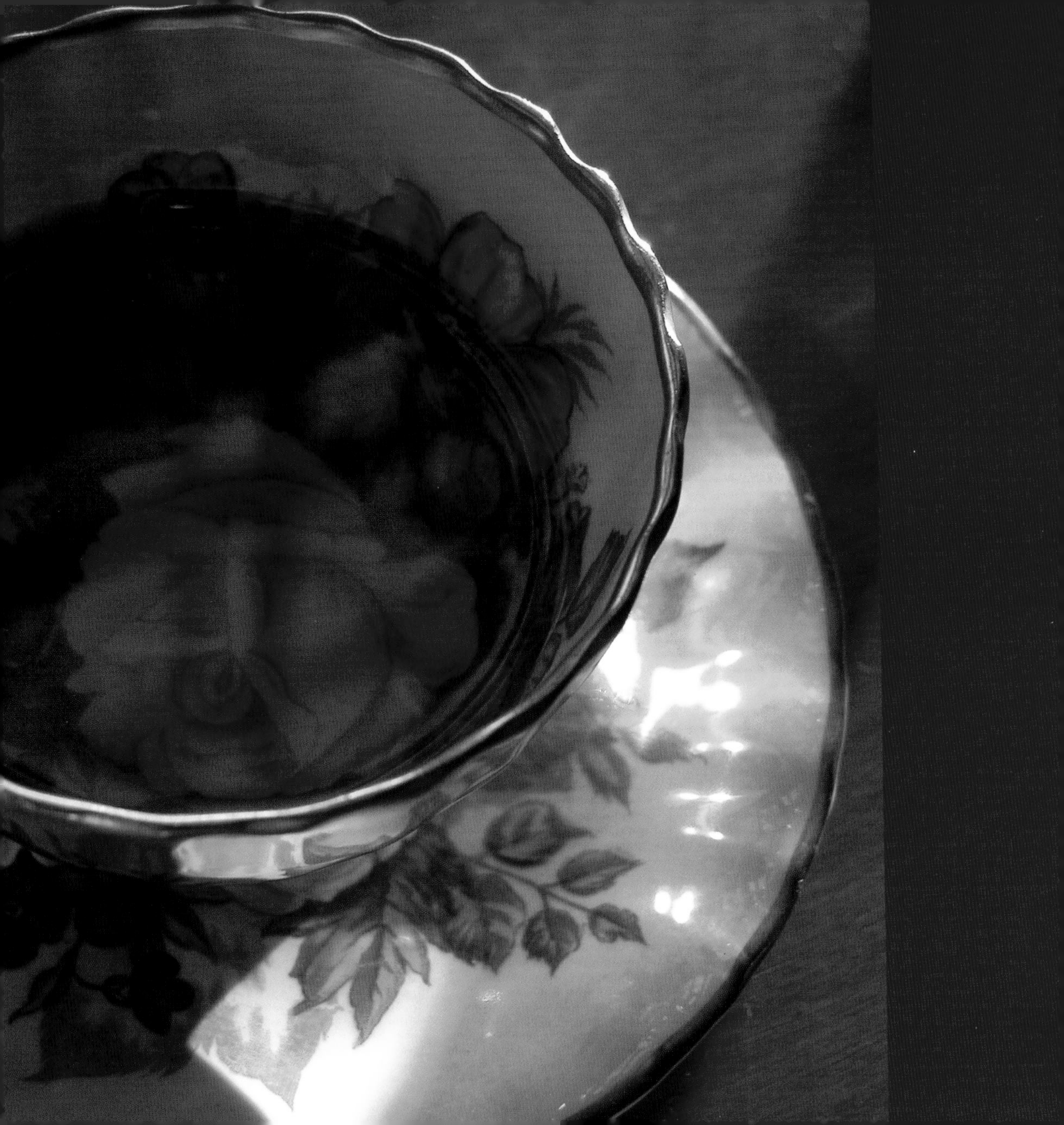

SUMATRAN MOONLIGHT

by Birgit Nielsen

Margaret worried whether she had brought enough coal briquets up from the cellar. Anna was coming for tea this afternoon. She couldn't remember the last time she had seen the girl, perhaps it was when Henrik, Anna's father, was still alive. Her beloved brother, who now lay buried in their childhood home near the Danish border. Always getting rained on in his small grey urn.

The girl was visiting from America and had specifically asked for tea when she called to announce her visit. Margaret drew in her breath sharply as she stared into the kitchen cabinet. Did the short grain rice have flies again? She thought she saw a flutter in the glass jar. She peered at the kernels. Nothing.

Henrik. Will. Bernhard. Men. These fleeting creatures. Oppressive, dominant like a trumpet solo and then the void. She turned the jar and squinted. Nothing.

Margaret spotted a tin of tea in the corner. Dusty. She wiped the lid with the cuff of her strawberry cardigan and pried it open, then raised the tin to her face and sniffed. It still had a smell to it, warm and bitter, a faint bit sweet and smoky.

On Sumatra, Will had taken the folded linen pouch from the breast pocket of his shirt. Margaret had thought then it was endearing of him to warm the tea leaves with the heat of his heart. He had opened the pouch to smell the tea's pungent fragrance. His meticulously combed hair, parted on the side, his impeccably shaven cheeks and jaw, the tiny beads of sweat that came to rest on his brow in the abominable heat of the tropics. The second time Margaret met with him—after he had delivered the terrible news of her mother's death—he, the unwilling harbinger, fellow prisoner of war albeit one with certain privileges, invited her back for tea and a game of chess. Perhaps he did not know how to alleviate her grief, for this time he held the pouch to her face to let her smell. He smiled as he did so.

Margaret replaced the lid on the tin and set it on the counter. Slowly, never taking her eyes off the tin, she closed the kitchen cabinet doors and mechanically turned the key to hold the doors in place. Will. Dear man. Dead, for sure, by now. She couldn't say how he had ensured that his stash never waned. For him, of course, tea was a lifeline. He was English after all and a colonel. Disciplined to a fault, he rationed his tea, brewing only a cup for each of them at the start of the game.

Margaret looked at the clock; it was nearly 4 P.M. Where was the girl? Visiting her mother and the family, Henrik's in-laws. Perhaps she didn't want to leave now; not surprising, having come so far to see them for the Christmas holiday and then having to leave to see Margaret.

She rubbed her palms together and pulled the cardigan tighter. As she picked up the kettle and filled it with water, she could see her breath. Must be chilly out. Poor girl, walking out in the cold.

Margaret rushed through the dark hallway into the living room at the end to check on the coal stove. If the girl didn't come soon, she'd have to go down to the cellar and bring up more briquets. Only a handful left for the night. One had to ration as one didn't know when times would turn again. She shoveled two more briquets into the gleaming nest of red and locked the stove door.

Perhaps she should run outside to see whether she could see her coming. Pick up some change on the way out, hurry down to the phone box at the corner to call over at the in-laws just to be sure the girl was still coming. She might otherwise be waiting and worrying for hours, and she resented the wait so very much.

She pulled on an extra pair of socks, got back into the felt slippers, grasped the ends of the cardigan sleeves as she slid her arms into the coat. Grabbed the keys and some change and the flashlight (wasteful to turn on the hallway lamp for the brief seconds it took to run down to the street) and hurried down the stairs.

Out in the street, she recognized the eerie shimmer. As if the whole world, even the gas station at the corner, had been dipped in a silver bath. It was a frosty, moonlit night. The felt slippers gave her no traction on the black ice forming on the sidewalk and she stopped. Wretched moon, relentless cold light.

The endlessness of moonlit nights in the tropics, the unforgiving heat on the clammy thin mattress. Silvery beams penetrated the bamboo siding, darkness striped with liquid shimmer and longing, interspersed only by fleeting moments of joy over one cup of tea and a game of chess. She didn't know why Will had wanted her company but was so pleased, so eager for his. Brief interludes infused with the fragrance from his pouch, a scent never replicated, so rich and civilized that all else disappeared: the uncouth smells of the jungle, the sweat, the stench of decomposition from plant and animal matter, the unaired mattress, the smell of burnt rubber, animal blood. Many nights alone, streaked in silvery light. What to do when all one could do was wait, not knowing?

She turned her head, glimpsed and covered her eyes quickly. It was big and bright. She peeked out between the fingers. No one on the street, no one walking toward the apartment building. Then she spotted a figure, a young woman perhaps? Difficult to tell these days since they all wore pants and square jackets. Perhaps it was Anna. She'd better get back inside and put the kettle on. It was unsafe to be out here in the cold, all by herself in the moonlight.

Inside, still in her coat, she rushed through the rooms to make sure the curtains were drawn on all windows. She would not sleep if the light shone in.

Margaret put a dish of sugar cubes and a tin of condensed milk on the tea tray. Did she still have cookies from last year? The armoire in the living room held her neatly compartmentalized stash: several packages of ginger snaps, Danish butter cookies, and crispy molasses. Henrik's favorite. *Braune Kuchen*. Perhaps his daughter had an affinity for them, too. Might run in the family.

Mother had given Mam'selle a hard time whenever the molasses cookies turned out too thick, soggy or burnt, too sweet, too bitter.

143

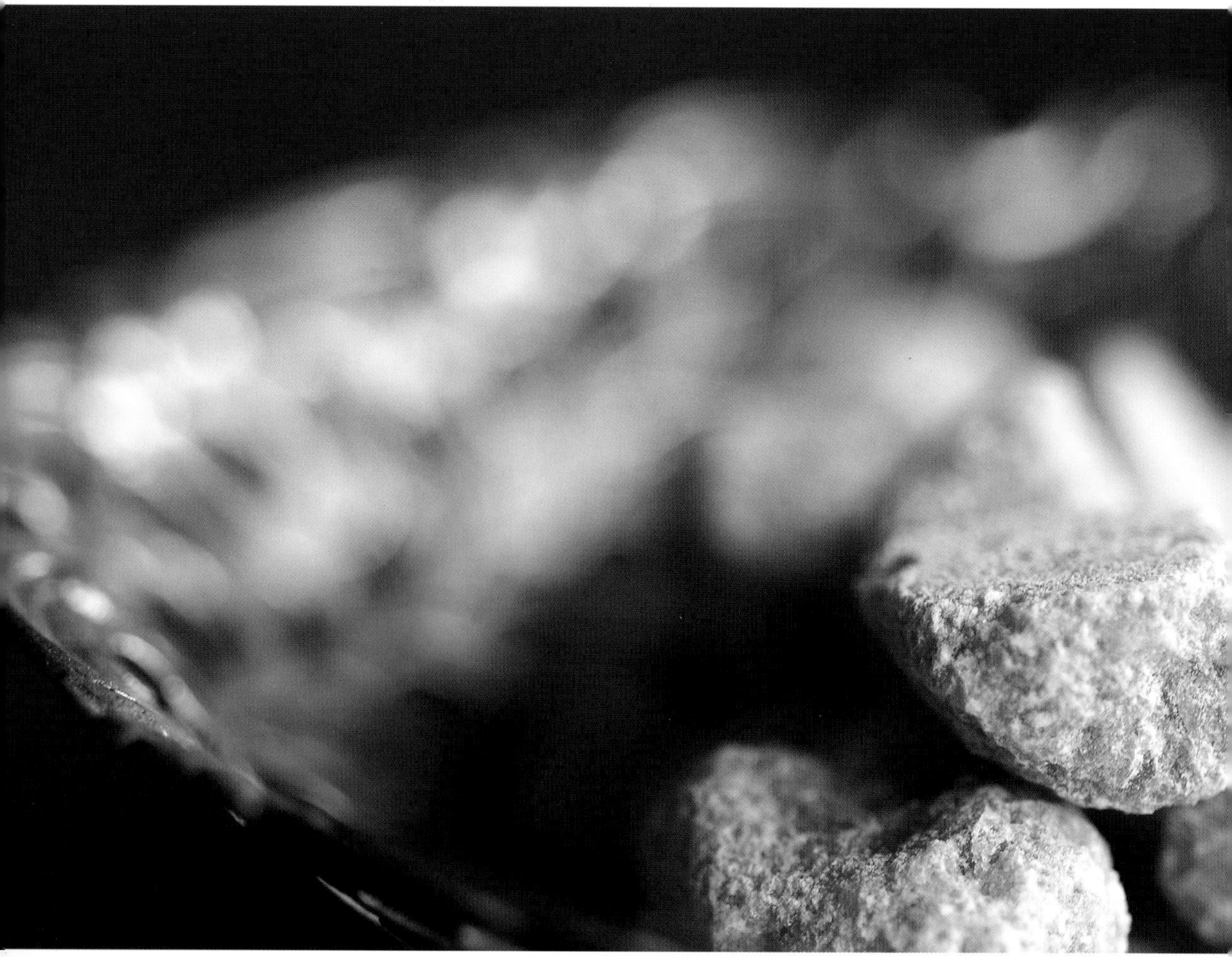

Mam'selle had served tea when Bernhard came at Christmas to ask for Margaret's hand. He ate molasses, chatted idly with Henrik, bowed to Father and left without another word. Returned a month later, a week before Margaret's birthday, to ask for Ella's, her little sister's, hand instead. A vase with snowdrops stood on the piano that day.

Margaret arranged the cookies on a chipped plate. The kettle was beginning to hum. She turned the gas down. If the person on the street was Anna, the doorbell should be ringing any second.

"What will become of you, Margaret," Mother had said, "what shall we do with you?"

Bernhard had recommended her for missionary duty as a way to rid himself of the embarrassment. Mother had looked to her husband and then her son, the newly ordained minister, for encouragement.

"A social duty, a calling to serve in the name of Luther," Henrik had said to his sister, hands behind his back, rocking on his heels. Henrik married Ella and Bernhard a week later.

And now they were all dead: Henrik, Ella, and Will. Only Bernhard was still alive.

The doorbell. There... there, the doorbell. The girl had meant to come after all.

"Oh, come in, dear, quick." She waved her hand into the brightly lit hall. The girl, smiling broadly, took her time coming up the stairs.

"Hurry, it's cold out."

Anna laughed. "I know. I just walked to get here."

"Shouldn't be out walking in the dark. It's dangerous."

"Oh, don't you worry about me, Aunt Margaret. I'm all right." The girl opened her arms to embrace Margaret.

The closeness startled Margaret and she stepped a little to the side. "So glad you came. Here, hang up your coat. Let's go into the salon, I've kept it nice and warm for you." After gently pushing Anna toward the living room, she hurried back into the kitchen to bring the water to a boil.

The door creaked in the hinges and the girl poked her head in. "Can I help? My God, Aunt Margaret, it's freezing in here."

Margaret chuckled, "Yes, well, I'm not here a lot, don't heat the place when it's empty. But let's not talk about me. Tell me about yourself."

The kettle whistled and she lifted it with a charred pot holder that Anna's mother had crocheted eighteen years before. The water sputtered into the pot. A strong, bittersweet scent drifted up. She placed the lid on the silver pot with its wobbly handle—Aunt Bertha's inheritance, an entire set with silver cup holders and crystal glasses all stashed in the armoire, silver spoons with engraved handles, the fine Danish blue & white, the red and gold bone china cups from Manila, all from Aunt Bertha, another traveler among the forgotten women.

Margaret retrieved two chipped enamel mugs from the cabinet. "Done. Let's go into the nice warm salon."

To make room for the tray on the mahogany table by the window, she shoved the stack of magazines into the curtain and tugged at the fabric. Wicked moonlight. Margaret sunk into the burgundy armchair. She reached under her thigh and adjusted the cushion to get herself comfortable over the shot spring, then placed her cold hands on her knees and looked at her niece. "How pretty you are. You're taking after your mother. You must miss her terribly now that you live so far away."

"It's no different than living in Copenhagen or Stockholm. The flight's longer, that's all." The girl smiled.

"Oh, I miss my mother. I shall never forget the last time I saw her."

"When was that?" Anna asked, tilting her head.

Margaret smoothed the seam of her dress. Chilly night. The knees ached. "Mother took me to the train station on my way to Sumatra. You know I was a missionary there, don't you?"

"Of course."

Margaret placed her hands on the armrests of the burgundy chair and lifted herself up. She hunched over the tray, took the lid off the pot and stirred. A rich malty smell rose with the steam. She placed the strainer over Anna's mug and poured. The liquid was as dark as coffee. Good strong tea, served only with a sliver of lemon and plenty of rock candy that tinkled in the cup when stirred. Too bitter without it. Tea that herring and shrimp fishermen on the northern coast drank with a shot of rum at night. Weathered faces under greasy battered skipper's caps. The visors on their caps dented over furrowed brows. East Frisian tea.

"Here," she said, "I'm just out of lemon. Have some sugar and condensed milk. And I have some *braune Kuchen*. Do you like them? Also Danish butter cookies. The best." Margaret smiled. "Danish butter has no match."

She adjusted the cushion beneath her. "The last time I saw Mother, I'd boarded the train in Berlin and was leaning out the window to the platform where Mother was. She looked old and small and she began to cry. Father was already dead. I couldn't understand then why she was crying. I kept saying to her not to worry, I'd be back before she knew it.

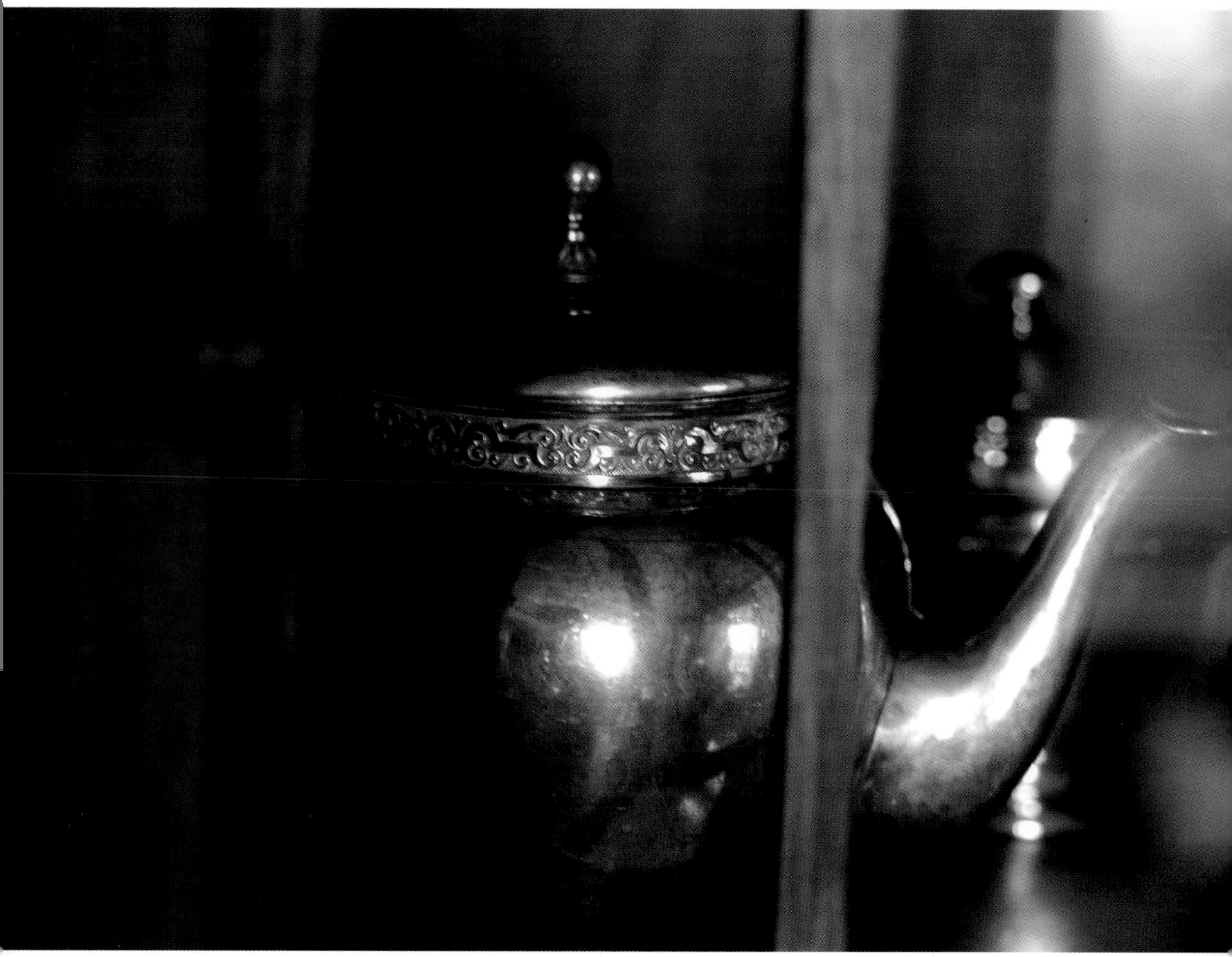

I only meant to go for two years. What's two years? Nothing. You're naive when you're young. I've often thought to myself over the years that she must have known we'd never see each other again."

Margaret stirred the tea and squeezed the lid of the punctured condensed milk can, releasing drop after drop into the tea while she stirred until it had reached the color of caramel. She placed three sugar cubes on the teaspoon and lowered it so the tea seeped into the cubes.

"Didn't you have any idea about the war coming?" Anna asked.

"How old are you now? Twenty four? When you leave and go back to America, do you think there might be a war and you'd never see or hear from your mother ever again? Not even a letter? Of course not. You're young, naïve. You think nothing bad will ever happen."

"How long were you in the camp?"

"Ten years, 1938 to '48." Margaret placed the spoon on her tongue, crushed the softened sugar against the roof of her mouth. "Sweet. So good."

Anna sipped from the mug. "When did you find out she had died?"

"In '41. She'd been dead a year. A British colonel told me. He had received word that Mother had died in 1940 and that I ought to be informed. Then he handed me a stack of my letters." She rested against the back of the armchair. "They were marked 'return to sender.' Dog-eared, wrinkled, damp to the touch, they had gone around the world and come back unopened. All my worries and my queries as to her health, how was she coping, had she heard from Henrik, nothing I had written ever reached her. It's a cruel life when a perfect stranger, an Englishman, has to tell you your mother is long gone and buried. And there's nothing you can do. You can't even go home."

"How come he told you? Was he in charge of the camp?"

"Goodness, no. He was a prisoner like myself. The Dutch incarcerated us both. They detested the English over Colonial squabbles and as soon as the war in Europe started, I was the enemy. We played chess."

"You played chess?"

Margaret laughed. "Yes, we had a game of chess now and then and we had tea. He said a lot of the inmates weren't very bright. Imagine."

"Would you ever go back?"

Margaret frowned, reached across to grab a molasses cookie, and dipped it into the tea. It was an art to get the cookie into your mouth without losing the soggy end. Henrik had been particularly good at it.

"Go back to Sumatra? Never. For one thing, the moon would be the end of me."

"The moon?" The girl's high-pitched laugh kicked over in its last note. "Why?" Anna reached for the cookies. She chose the Danish butter cookies, Margaret noted.

How inquisitive, the young. Always asking questions, wanting answers. "I got very sick from the moonlight in Sumatra. You couldn't escape it. When it lit up the jungle it was like daylight. I never did manage to sleep. It made me sick. You mark my words. You be careful with the moon, you hear?"

Anna lowered her head, pressed her chin against her chest and peered up at her. A mocking smile formed on the girl's lips.

"Go ahead and laugh at me. I was not much older than you are today when it happened. I'd always loved the moon. There's something about the moonlight in the tropics though that's not right. I remember walking back to the bamboo shack after a game of chess. It was a clear warm night and the moon was out. The air smelled sweet. Something was in bloom, I suppose. I remember the sound of my feet on the ground. I stopped and looked up at the moon; it was enormous, a full moon but bigger, brighter than I had ever seen it. It almost blinded me. I didn't feel well when I returned to the barracks. I was nauseous, a little dizzy, and because we had no curtains, the light came in the entire night. It was frightening. And it never got better. In fact, it got much worse."

"Insomnia. Is that what it is?"

"Yes and no. Somnambulism. Sleepwalking."

Anna smiled. She sipped from her mug. Margaret noticed there was benevolence now in the girl's smile.

Anna placed the mug back on the table. "You weren't in love by any chance, Aunt Margaret?"

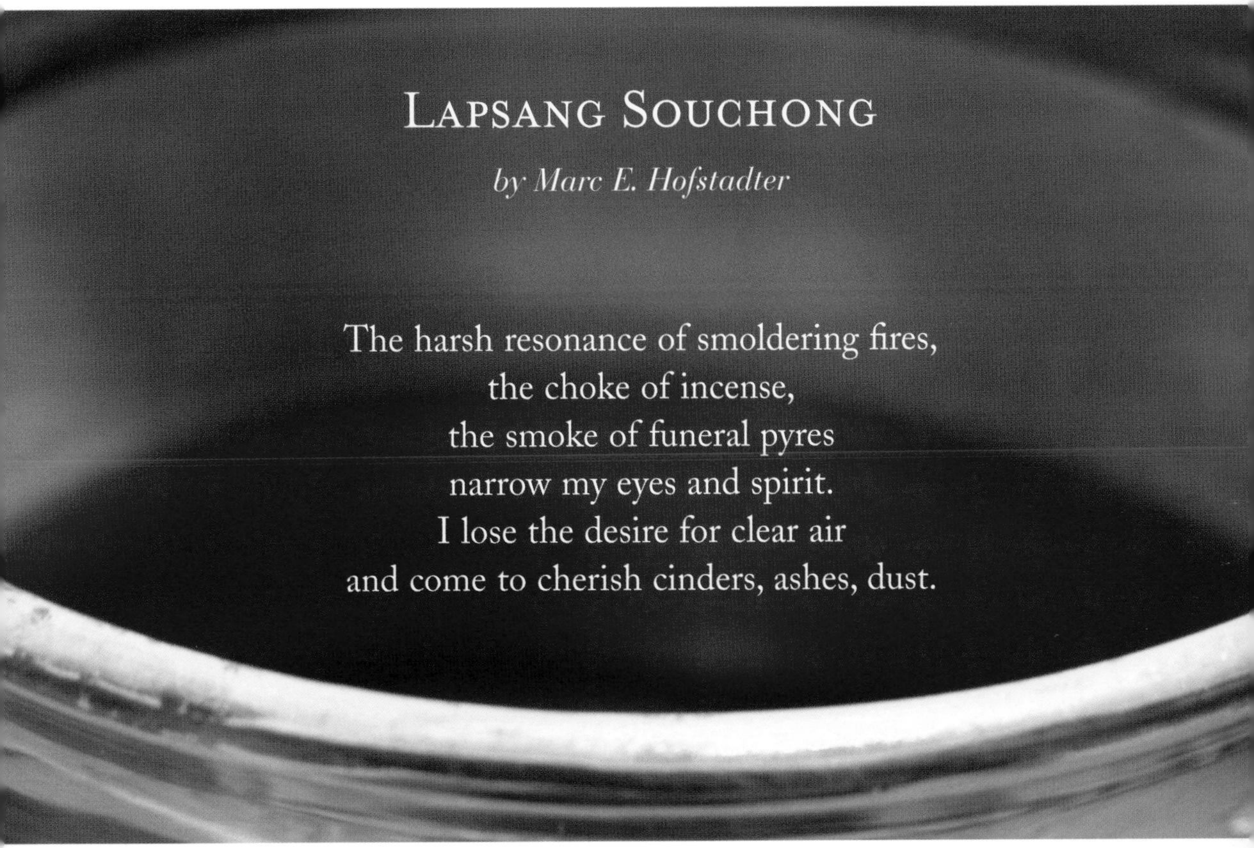

Lapsang Souchong

by Marc E. Hofstadter

The harsh resonance of smoldering fires,
the choke of incense,
the smoke of funeral pyres
narrow my eyes and spirit.
I lose the desire for clear air
and come to cherish cinders, ashes, dust.

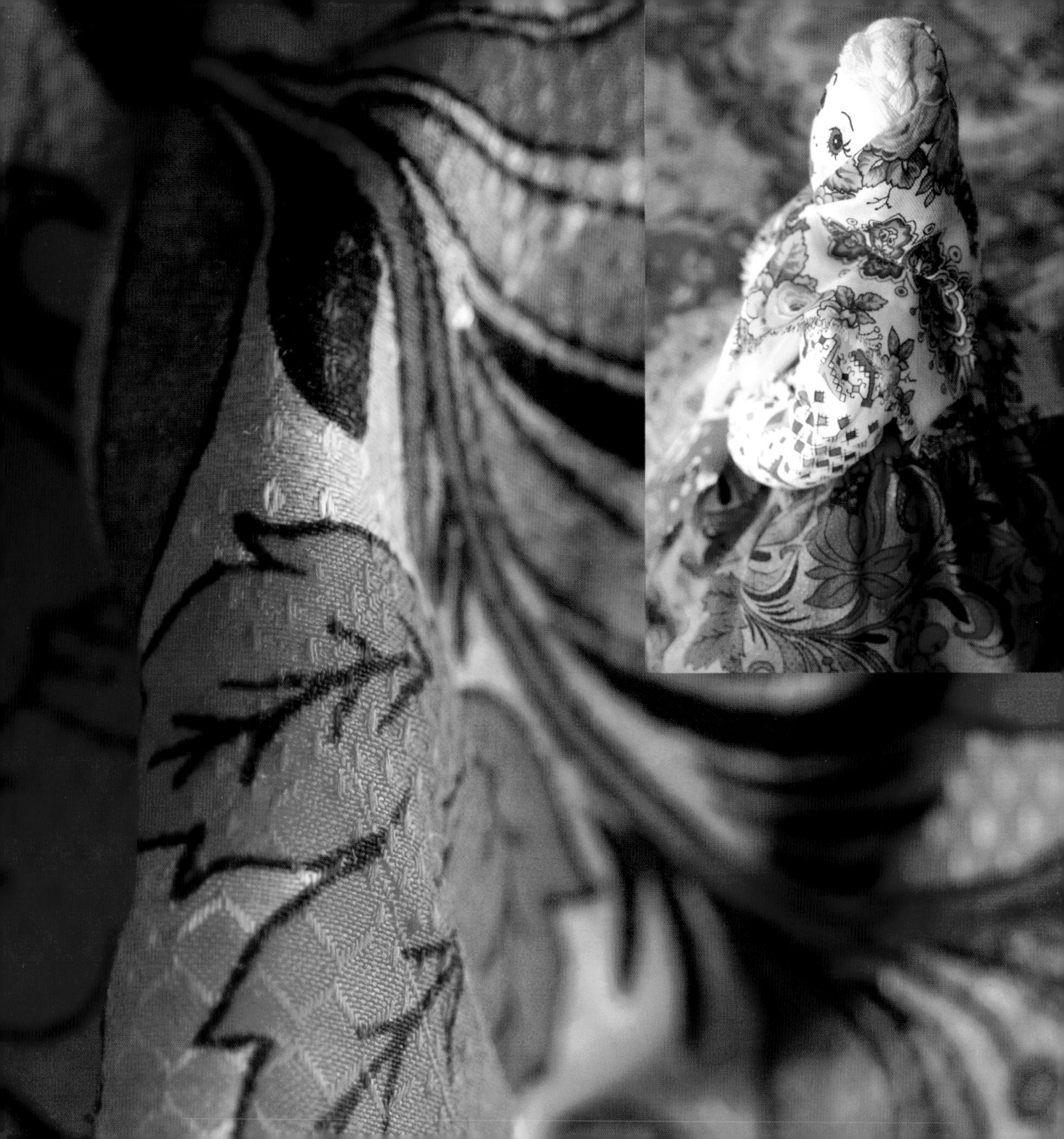

TELL ME SOMETHING GOOD

by Frances Saunders

"When I was a child in Odessa, with snow piled high on the rooftop, I don't remember so many colds. Don't be stubborn. Take a glesele." Mom's steaming glass of tea with lemon is a cure that costs much less than a doctor's visit.

After school, I walk home to a street of red brick Manhattan

tenements, enter the same building I've lived in since I was born, thirteen years ago. I race through the stale cooking odors trapped in the hallway, up two flights.

Mom's at the stove. She greets me with a toast, sloshing lemon and swirling tea leaves while stirring soup with her other hand.

"Mom, when you finish drinking please read my fortune."

"Absolutely not. How often have I told you, you're too young? Fortunes are games of hope grown-ups play."

"Okay, then teach me how, and I'll read my own leaves."

"You need an older head to figure out what the tea leaves show.

It's not always this or that. It's how the fortune teller sees them."

"What do you mean?" I tug on her apron.

"Some other time. Fold the wash before Pop comes home for supper."

The following day after school, I see Mom at the corner, weighed down with shopping bags. "I saw Bessie Roth down the street," she tells me. "Every time she looks inside a baby carriage, her eyes get so big it breaks my heart. I told her to invite the other women here for tea on Thursday. We'll schmooze and eat cake, and maybe I'll read tea leaves."

All day Thursday the classroom clock moves like thickened honey. During recess I boast to my teacher, "My Mom's reading tea leaves this afternoon."

She looks like I've swung a dead rat in her face and says, "I hope one day soon you'll realize that in this country we don't put our trust in foreign superstitions." I want to tell her that Mom's got more brains than she'll ever have, but it's risky talking back to a teacher, and besides, a lump in my throat chokes off the words.

I rush home after school and find a yeast cake, lemon wedges, and sugar cubes arranged on our best white tablecloth. Tea steeps in a gold-rimmed china pot, and water simmers on the stove. The tea

glasses gleam. The house has the scrubbed, quiet feel of Friday night.

"Mom, you're gorgeous in your good green dress." Her eyes glow in her party face. The doorbell growls. Mrs. Klein's bulk fills the doorway.

Mom and Mrs. Klein whisper on our lumpy couch. Mrs. Klein's swollen ankles spill over her laced shoes, and I vow my legs will never look like hers.

Again the doorbell. It's Mrs. Miller, my favorite neighbor, baby Esther in her arms. Mom takes the infant into her bedroom, crooning a lullaby, and lowers her on the wide bed. Mrs. Miller sheds her coat, tosses her knitted hat on the bureau, and finger-combs her bobbed hair. We waltz into the living room singing, "I'm forever blowing bubbles." Despite her jiggly bosoms, I think she's the beauty queen of all the tea drinkers.

Mrs. Winter, whom Mom nicknamed "the bird," arrives next, wiping her beaky nose. Her old maid sister Clara stands behind her. I dump their coats on Mom and Pop's bed.

By the time Mrs. Roth makes her entrance, Mom's slicing the cake. Mrs. Roth slips off her black Hudson seal fur coat, hands it to me with a "be a nice girl." She adjusts the combs in her auburn hair, then lowers herself into a chair beside Clara. I once told Mom that Mrs. Roth reminded me of a pear, skinny on top and fat on the bottom. Mom scolded me, but the corners of her eyes crinkled.

I hide in a dim corner of the living room where I can spy. Mom, her face flushed, refills glasses, and offers cake. Outstretched hands reach to touch her as if she's a lucky charm. "Lena," they say, "what would we do without you."

Mom throws her head back and laughs. "It's the tea leaves, not me."

When the jabbering bounces off the walls, and no one seems to be listening to anyone else, Mom claps. "Come, everyone. Move closer.

Who wants to go first?" The women look at their shoes like shy brides.

"Clara, how about you?" Mom says. Clara, mousy in her long gray dress, hands Mom her glass and mumbles, "Who needs a wife with wrinkles?"

"Don't be so sure, Clara," Mom cautions, rolling the glass between her hands. She peers inside, her forehead pleated with effort. The tea leaves can't turn Clara into a fairy princess, but Mom calls this a game of hope. I wait breathlessly.

"I see a respectable-looking older gentleman, maybe a widower, in a jacket and tie." Mom tilts the glass, squints as if to see better. "I make out a small shape beside him. It could be his grandchild."

"From your mouth to God's ears," Clara's sister says.

"So who else has a problem?"

"Who doesn't?" Mrs. Klein heaves her heavy bosom and gives her nose a hard blow. Heads turn in her direction. "You already know my *tsuris*. As soon as I..." She pats her stomach, "Sol took off like the wind."

Mom studies her tea leaves, rolls her eyes to heaven, silently moves her mouth as if seeking divine help. Mrs. Klein fidgets with her wedding ring. After another shake of the glass, Mom's face brightens. "I see a cradle, and a rocking chair. Also a needle and a spool of thread."

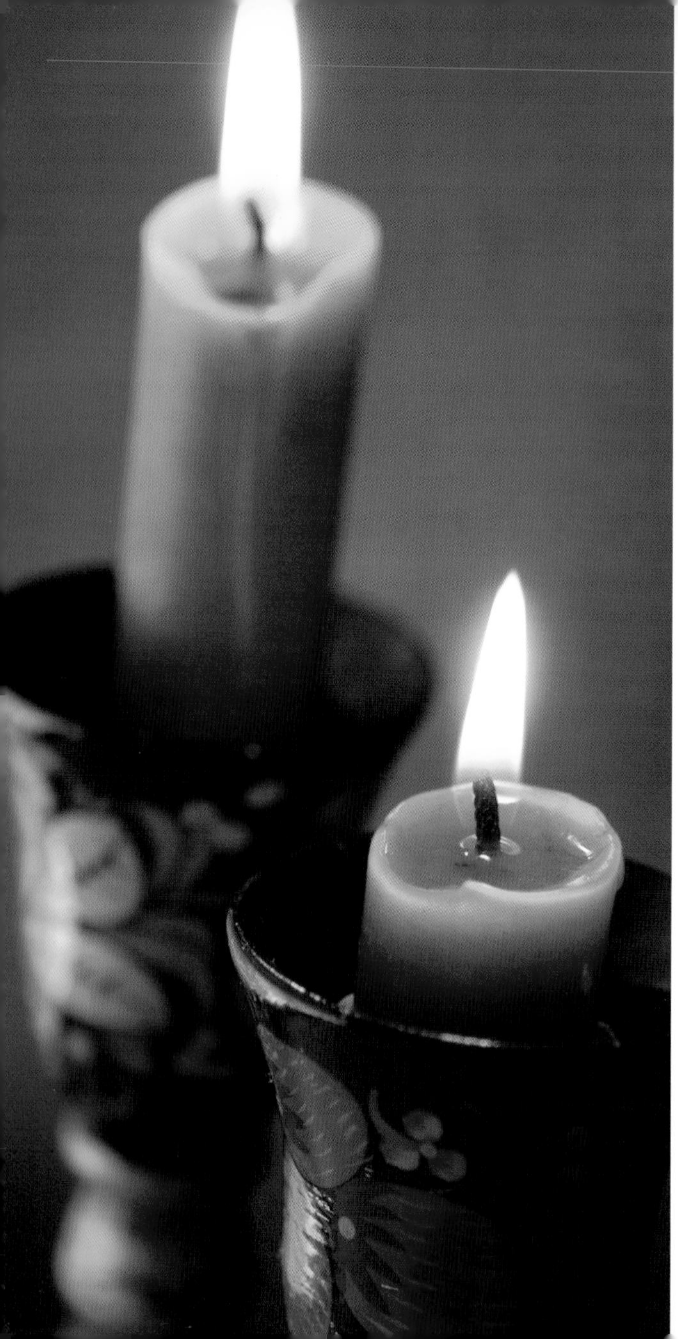

"Oh, Lena. I'll take in sewing and my mother will help with the baby. You've taken a heavy stone from my heart. At least I'll have a daughter in my old age."

"Klein," my mother grins, "the tea leaves can do just so much. But if it's a son, he'll marry and either way, you'll win." There's a burst of laughter, as though the sun peeped from behind a black cloud. Mrs. Klein tries a weak smile on her blotchy face. When the women take a break, Mrs. Roth lingers by her side, gently touches her arm.

I sneak a piece of cake, my thoughts going around like a carousel. Do the tea leaves ever refuse to take shape, or scare the players with bad news?

After the women settle themselves again, Mrs. Miller passes her glass to Mom. "Lena, tell me something good. Sam's laid off again. It's slow season for pressers. I've asked my folks for a loan, but they don't even have enough for themselves."

Mom bites her lip, gazes solemnly into the distance. Perhaps she's worried Pop might lose his job too? Mrs. Miller clears her throat, and Mom snaps out of her daydream. She rests the glass on the table, sweeps her hands in the air like over shabbos candles, then lowers her head to read. I close my eyes. Please, tea leaves, be kind to Mrs. Miller.

Mom says, "I see boxes side by side. Let's hope they're packed full with work." The baby's whimpering. Mrs. Miller jumps up to nurse her, first bending to brush Mom's cheek with a kiss.

"Now me!" Mrs. Roth almost shouts. "Here's my glass." Her eyes sweep the group as though she's about to deliver a speech. "I don't know where to begin. I need new furniture, a vacation, an up-to-date fur coat." Her shoulders slump. Her voice drops as if she's losing steam. "My husband Morris promised to buy me a diamond dinner ring for our anniversary. But where is it? Lena, maybe the leaves show the ring on another woman's finger." Mrs. Roth wants so much from the tea leaves. Why, I wonder.

Mom caresses the glass against her cheek, gazes at Mrs. Roth before covering the top with her palm. Then, ever so slowly, she exposes the tea leaves. As soon as she lowers her eyes to look, her head pulls back, and her mouth tugs down at the corners. Dead quiet settles in the room. The women lean forward. My stomach knots with fear. Mrs. Roth's quavering voice breaks the silence. "What's taking so long?"

"Look at the clock," Mrs. Winter says. "It's almost supper time." The women begin their usual lengthy good-byes, hugging and kissing, loud and joyful. All but Mrs. Roth, who clings to Mom.

"Please Lena, I won't rest until I know what you saw in my glass."

Mom's arm circles Mrs. Roth's waist, draws her closer. "Bessie, I saw nothing, with nothing. Scattered pieces without form. I know you're disappointed, but as long as friends come together, there are always more chances. Go and be well."

After Mrs. Roth leaves, Mom lights the stove under the pot of prakas and hurries to change back into herself in her old brown wool dress and long apron. I lick the crumbs off the cake plates, and we straighten the living room. The last chair in place, I playfully pull Mom down on the couch.

"What did you really see in Mrs. Roth's glass? I promise I won't tell."

She searches my face with her tired one. "Up until Mrs. Roth, all the women had a little piece of hope to carry home. But tea leaves do what they want, and something told me our good fortune might not last. I forced myself to look, and what I saw gripped me..." She stands.

"Please." I yank on her apron. "You haven't finished. Did the leaves say Mrs. Roth is being punished because she's greedy?"

Mom lifts my chin, and looks deep into my eyes. "No, Mrs. Roth's a good soul. She'd give up all her foolish desires if only she was blessed with a child. I saw an overturned cradle half buried in the wet leaves, and I didn't have the heart to send a friend home with the bitter taste of gall."

"What happened to the baby?"

Mom turns toward the kitchen. "It wasn't meant to be."

I look out at the dark street lit by the comer street lamp, comforted by the pungent aromas of supper. As I wait for Pop, I replay the long afternoon and think about how Mom wrestled with the tea leaves, about how with reading fortunes come risks.

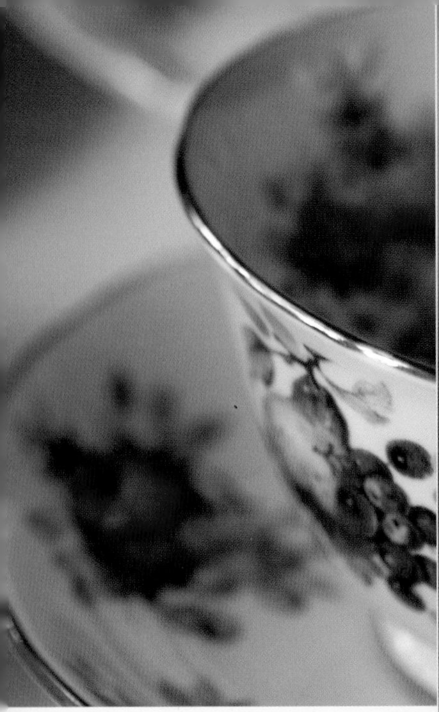
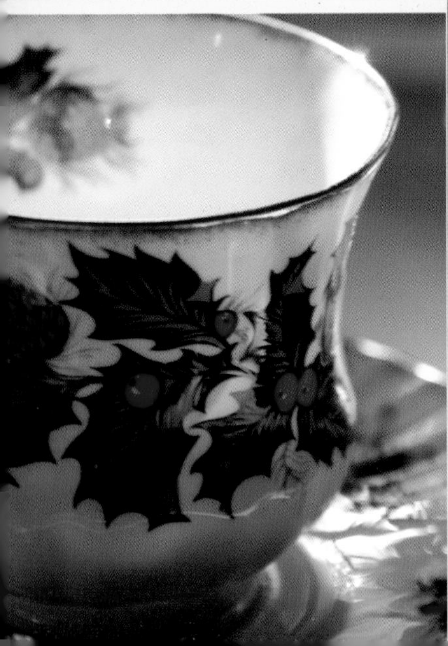
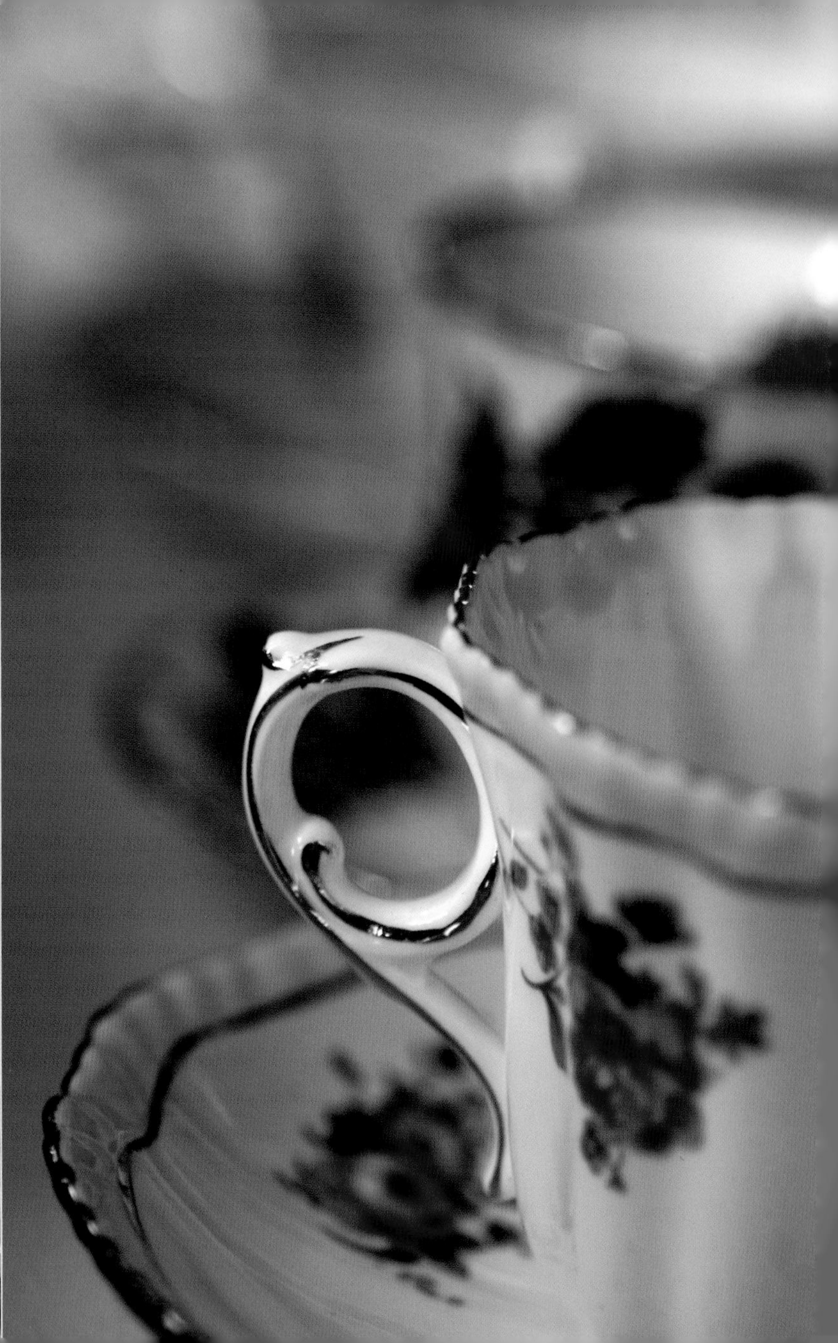

Tea Cups and Christmas Angels

by Tolbert McCarroll

St. Luke's story of the first Christmas Eve is well known. I like Luke as a writer but I doubt things happened quite as he put it down.

It's the sheep that bother me. Remember how there were shepherds watching their flocks? *The angel of the Lord appeared to them. And the glory of the Lord shone around them.* And later, there appeared this *throng of the heavenly host* singing like some great Bach choir. What were the sheep doing all this time? The ones I see in the fields around my home will run when a rabbit hops along. Think what would happen if they saw *the glory of the lord* shining all about like some firework display and then were confronted with a blaring *throng of the heavenly host*. The shepherds would be chasing them all over the countryside. None of those fellows would have made it to Bethlehem that night!

Oh, I think there were shepherds at the crib. The whole point was for the simple, poor, humble, close-to-the-earth folk to get to the divine child before the mighty, wise, rich, sweet-smelling kings. Jesus came as a sort of refugee, not as a powerful monarch. We are being nudged to look for God in quiet places, not in citadels of wealth and power.

I also think angels, quiet unseen angels, got the shepherds to Bethlehem. They worked on the shepherds just as they will work on us every Christmas Eve. The angels' task was to get them to stop thinking about wolves, the price of wool, girlfriends, a good meal, and all the other thoughts which come into a person's mind in the stillness of the night. Then, in that brief empty space, to encourage them to accept that there might be something of great significance in the little things around them. Such as a light coming from the stable.

With all the busyness surrounding secular and religious activities, it is easy to miss the point of this special night—for many, the most sacred and enchanting evening of the year. Years ago some exasperated angel pushed our family at Starcross to have a Christmas Eve Tea. Whatever is undone at that point is to remain undone! Lists of tasks are thrown away. Christmas begins.

We gather around the hearth at 2 P.M., which is midnight in Bethlehem. Like any family we share songs and memories. At some point sister Julie brings out a prized little tea set. It had belonged to Tina,

168

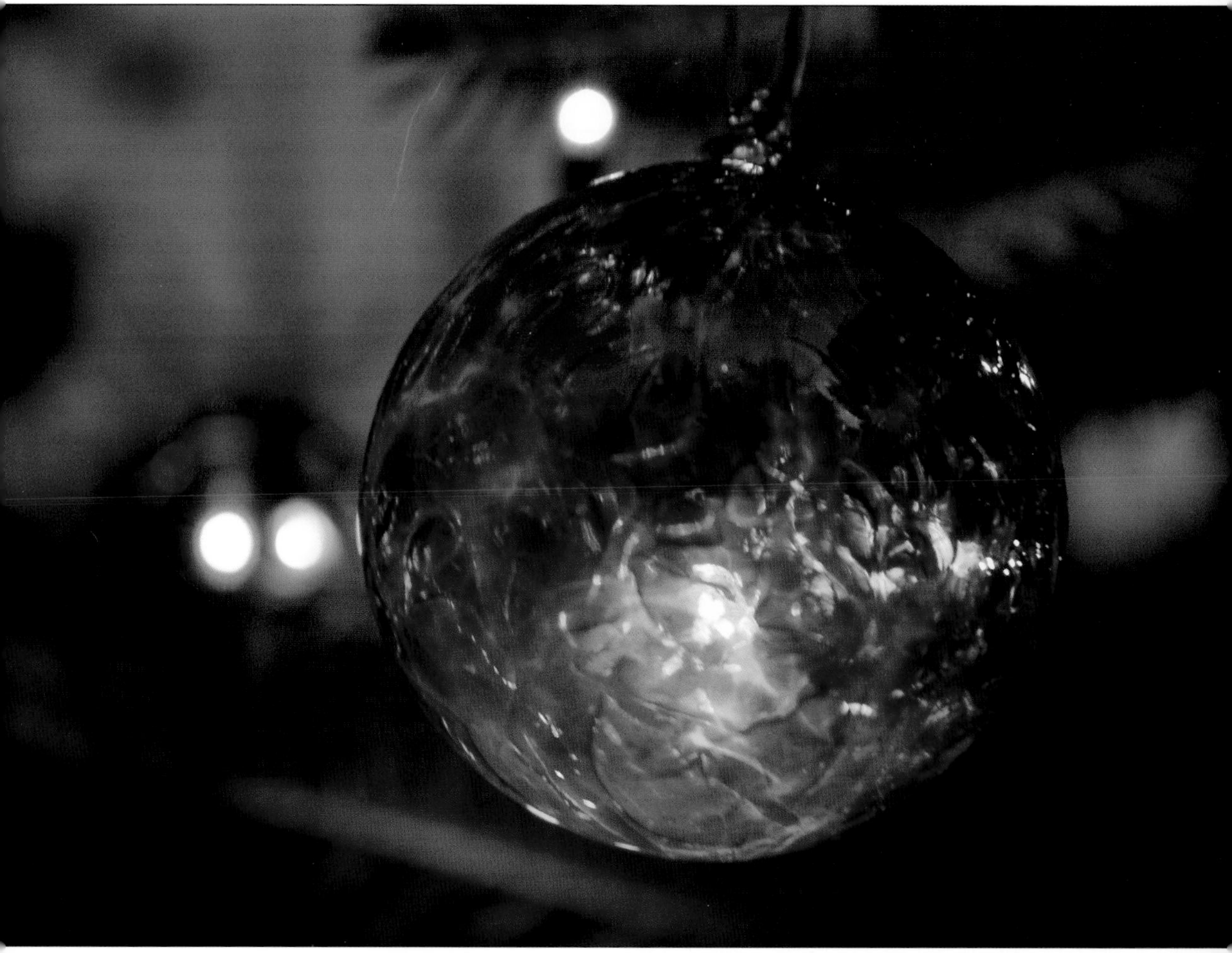

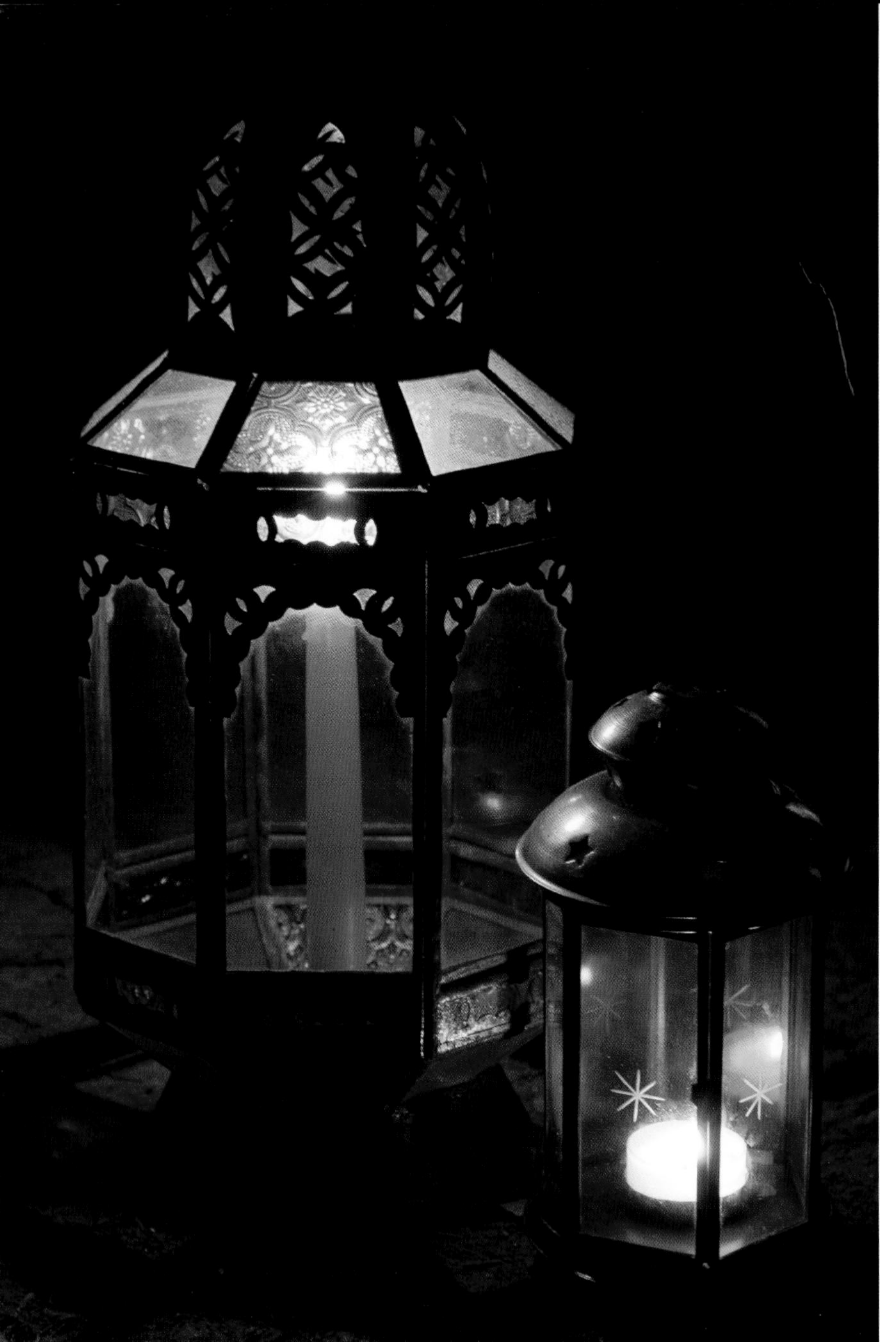

our adopted daughter who died from AIDS just before she was three.

On Christmas Eve Tina was very ill. Julie and sister Marti had rushed her from our farm to the hospital in Santa Rosa, a trip of about two hours. Late in the afternoon they called me. It looked very bad, they said. There was some chance she would not last the night. I put down the phone and turned around. There were our four other kids sitting on the couch looking at me. Our family has many Christmas Eve traditions and the children were old enough to expect them. What was going to happen with Tina, or with Christmas?

The high point of our Christmas Eve is when we each take a lantern and walk quietly under the stars up the hill to our little chapel. We had agreed that Marti and Julie would recite the same prayers and sing the same songs as we did in the chapel. This reassured the children. I was feeling considerable tension between my personal grief, this might be Tina's last night of life, and celebrating with the children the birth of new life. But we made it and the children went to bed with peace and expectations of the morning. At the hospital Tina was in a deep sleep.

Marti, Julie, and I were on the phone when our old clock tolled midnight. We read together a favorite passage from the Bible:

When peaceful silence lay over all,
and night had run the half of her swift course,
down from the heavens, from the royal throne,
leapt your all-powerful Word...
                    —*The Book of Wisdom 18:14*

172

We wished each other a blessed Christmas and prayed for Tina and all those families keeping watch over their children that night. Julie had in her backpack a small bottle of Grand Marnier for an eggnog that never got made. There were no glasses. But, for some reason, Tina's favorite toy tea set had come with her to the hospital. Solemnly, standing on either side of Tina, Julie and Marti poured the liqueur into the tiny cups and drank a toast. We have always felt the Holy Family, and an angel or two, joined in that toast.

Tina recovered the next day. Our family was reunited for a few more precious months. We have been drinking out of Tina's tea set every Christmas Eve since then. We have no doubt that Tina and a few celestial friends are always lifting a tiny cup with us.

I know that every family, couple, and person has a need for a Christmas Eve reprieve from the hectic pace of holiday life. And, every woman, man, and child has memories and traditions that broaden our spiritual horizons when shared on this special night. If you feel an urge to just drop all the unfinished tasks, then (and I choose my words carefully) for heaven's sake do it! You are probably being prodded by an angel impatiently waiting for Tea Time to begin in your house.

After all, even a Christmas angel can do with a quiet little break for tea.

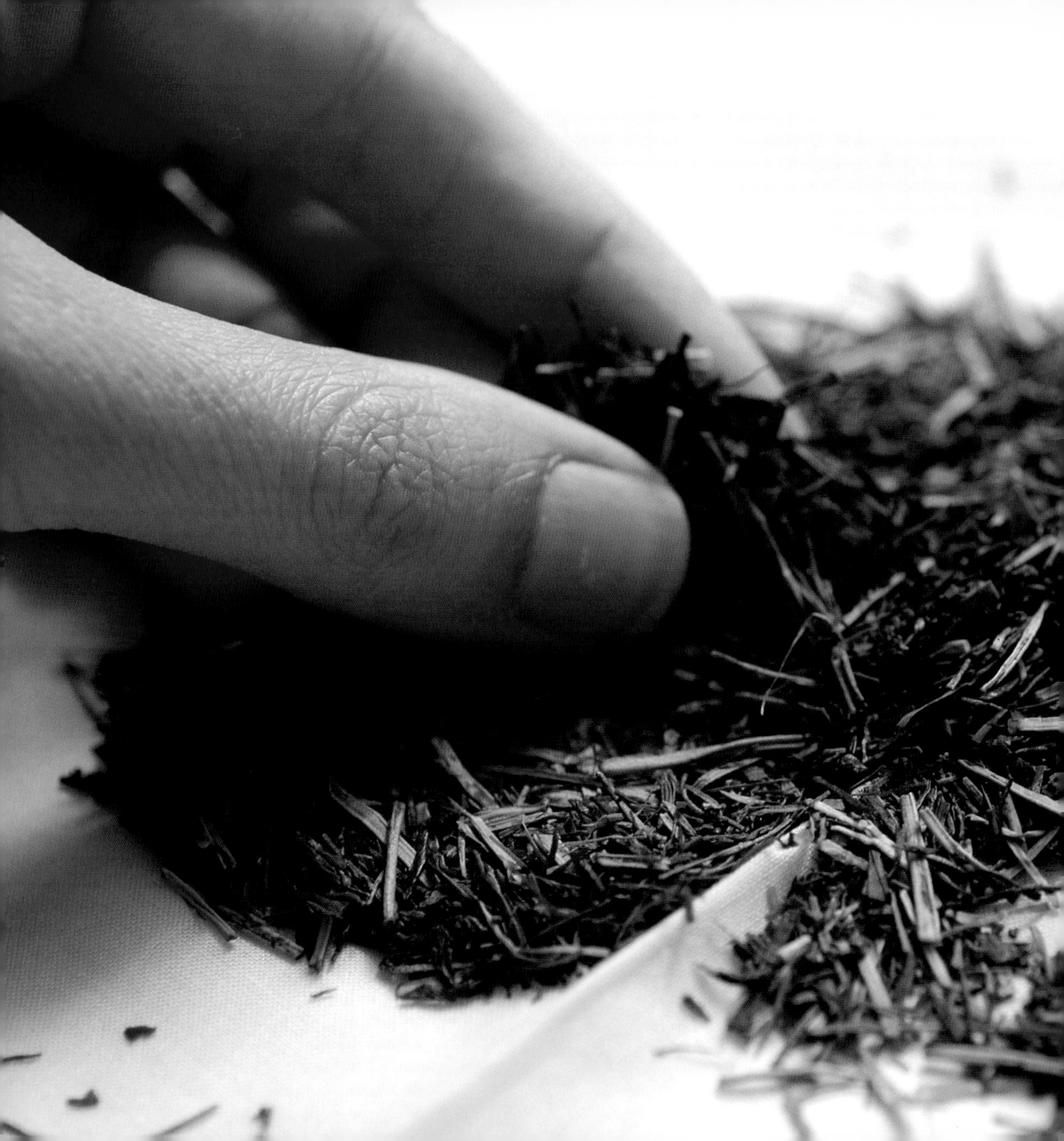

Making a Cup of
Green Tea, I Stop the War

by Stephen Levine

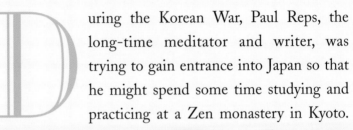

During the Korean War, Paul Reps, the long-time meditator and writer, was trying to gain entrance into Japan so that he might spend some time studying and practicing at a Zen monastery in Kyoto. But at this time Japan was being used as a military staging ground for the air battle and troop movement to the Korean War. Nonmilitary Westerners were not given visas. When he filed the necessary documents with the Asian immigration officer, he was told it would not be possible for him to visit Japan as he was not "militarily allied." Sitting opposite the immigration officer, he turned his visa request over and on the back wrote, "Making a cup of green tea, I stop the war," and handed it back to the official across the desk. The immigration officer took a long look at the poem, reading it silently to himself, "Making a cup of green tea, I stop the war." Turning the paper over, he initialed approval for Reps' entry into Japan. Looking up, he said, "We need more people like you in our country right now."

What does it mean to make a cup of green tea that stops the war? Reps wasn't being clever, he was being real. He was speaking of meeting the incessant struggle for control, our long-conditioned inner conflicts, with something other than old mind's old ways of violence and "victory," of mercilessness and inner strife. To make a cup of tea that doesn't continue the war, that doesn't deepen the conflict, the impatience, the waiting, the desire for things to be otherwise, one simply lets the water boil. Have we ever simply let the water boil?

Once, after sharing this story with a group, a fellow moved gradually toward me supported by a walker. His body had thinned to a near skeletal form. He looked up at me with sparkling eyes and said, "Dying of cancer, I stop the war." We stood together in a pool of silence. He wasn't backing away from cancer or anything else in his life. He told me how pain had taught him that any escape just increased the war. He was no longer at war with himself or with anything else. He was just dying of cancer.

176

How often do even our spiritual practices stop the war? Or do we make them just another holy war, another battle in the name of healing the mind and body? The more we see the mercilessness and fear in the mind, the less we add to the mercilessness in the body we all share, in the universe each of us inhabits. Seeing how unloving the mind can be, I stop the war. Sipping at the nectar of existence, I stop the war. Drinking a cup of green tea, I stop the war.

—*Adapted from* Healing into Life and Death

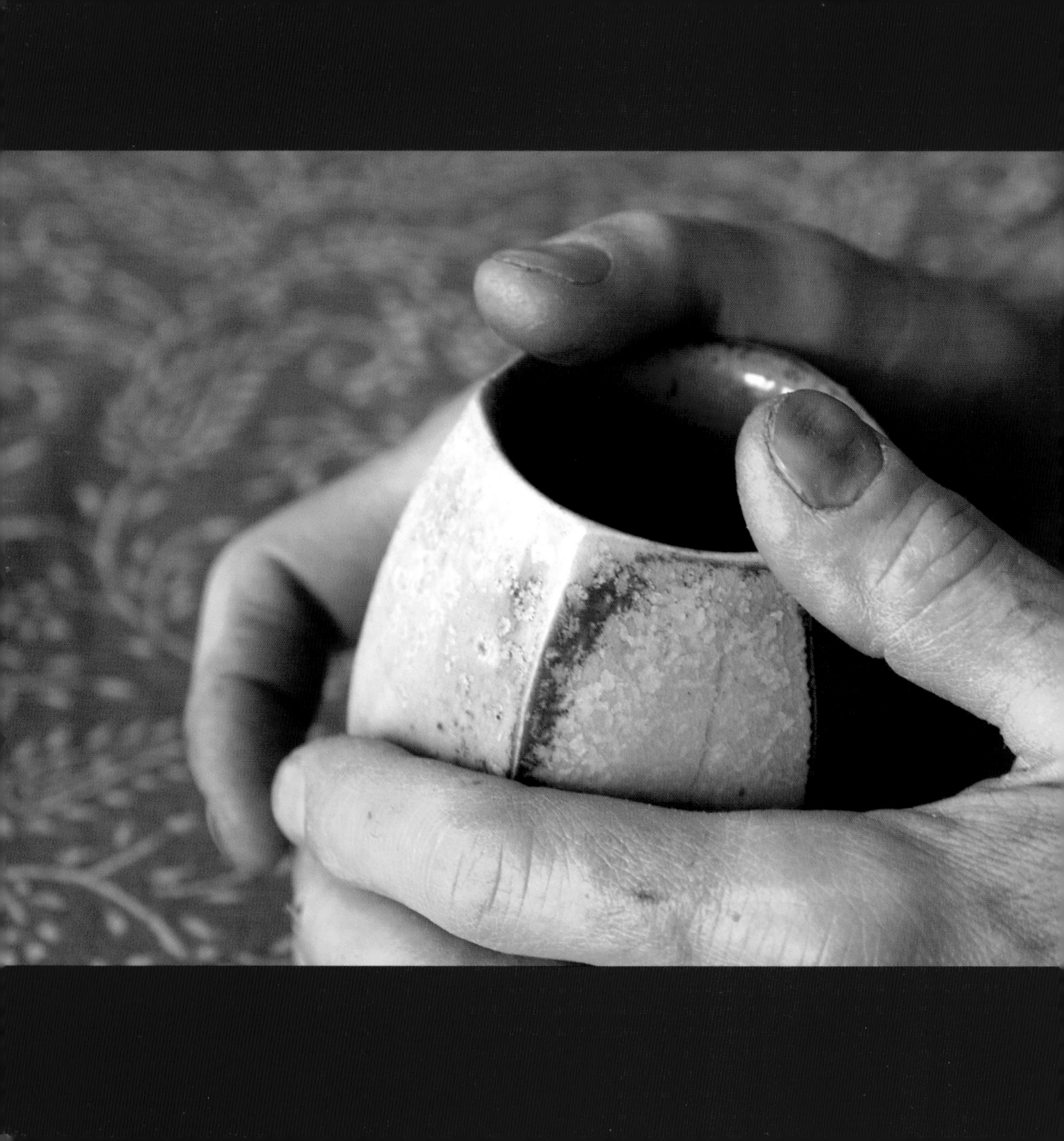

Ti Kuan Yin

by Marc E. Hofstadter

You hold me gently as a monk
cradles a prayer book,
lift me as a breeze
lofts a cloud.
I'm in your care.
We float through the afternoon.

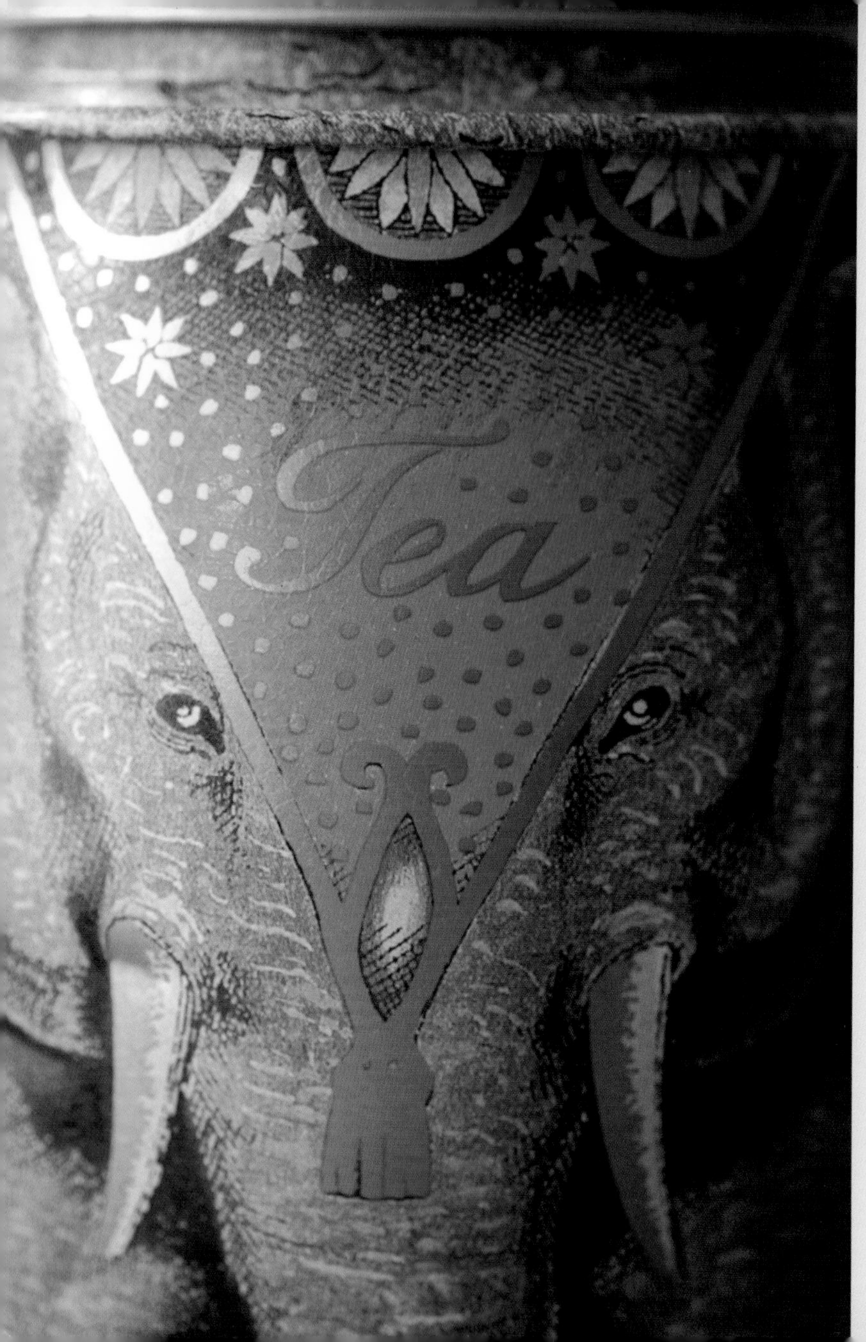
Tea

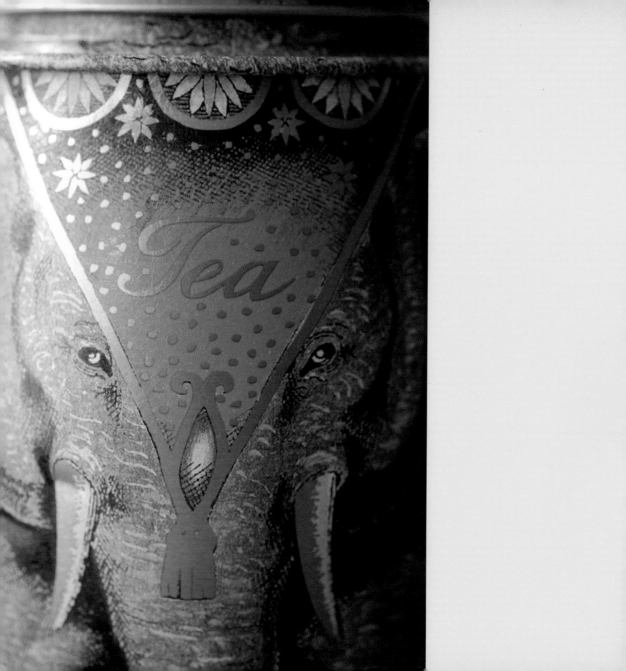

About the Writers

Lorraine Ash is a New Jersey journalist, playwright, and essayist for whom iced tea is one of life's constant little pleasures. She is the author of *Life Touches Life: A Mother's Story of Stillbirth and Healing*, with a foreword by Dr. Christiane Northrup; NewSage Press, 2004.

Sharon Bard is a writer who produces radio interviews and documentaries for public radio in Sonoma County, California. She has two cats, a doctorate in holistic health sciences, and has sipped tea in dozens of countries.

Susan Muaddi Darraj is a freelance writer whose work has appeared in "Baltimore Magazine," "Pages," "Calyx," "Sojourner," "New York Stories," and elsewhere.

Arthur Dobrin is Professor of Humanities at Hofstra University, Hempstead, New York and Leader Emeritus of the Ethical Humanist Society of Long Island.

D.L. DuBois grew up in Mississippi where tea comes over ice, lived in Kenya and drank it British style with milk and sugar, and now travels to tea plantations with her Sikh husband to enjoy it at its roots.

Meredith Escudier is a native Californian who has lived in France for over twenty-five years. She translates and writes, has been published in Parisian literary journals, and is currently working on a collection of essays.

Judith Grey is an English teacher in Baltimore County who writes her poetry in the summer on an island in Maine.

Saumya Arya Haas has been writing personal essays and fiction, drawing from her spiritual background and her experiences living in America, India and England.

Marc E. Hofstadter has a Ph.D. in Literature from U.C. Santa Cruz and has taught American literature there, at the Université d'Orléans, and at Tel Aviv University. He has published two books of poetry, *House of Peace* and *Visions*.

Stephen Levine is a pioneer in the field of conscious death and dying, author of many books on the topic, and has offered, together with his wife Ondrea, a free, nationwide 24-hour telephone hot line to counsel the dying and bereaved.

Tolbert McCarroll is a monk at the Starcross Community in Annapolis, California. He has adopted several children and directed children support programs in the US, Romania, and Uganda.

Birgit Nielsen is a writer, translator, perpetual student, traveler, and virtual resident of Germany, England, and California. She received an MFA from Goddard College.

Emily North lives in Brattleboro, Vermont, with her three children and teaches at the Community High School. She received an MFA from Goddard College in 2003.

Noreen Quinn-Singh grew up in Ireland and now lives in a Paris suburb with her Indian husband. She has published poems and short stories and is writing a book about her experiences in India.

Mariana Romo-Carmona is the author of *Living at Night and Speaking like an Immigrant*. Her book in Spanish, *Conversaciones*, won the 2002 Lambda Book Award. Born in Chile, she is a New Yorker who loves chocolate and the martial arts. She teaches in the Goddard College MFA Program and at Queens College in Manhattan.

Clara Rosemarda, writer, counselor, and workshop leader, teaches creative writing internationally. She lives and dances in Northern California.

Habeeb Salloum is a Canadian freelance writer specializing in Canadian, Arab, and Latin American history, travel, and the culinary arts.

Frances Saunders is a teacher, traveler, and tea drinker. She writes from Miami.

Marguerite Thoburn Watkins was born in the foothills of the Himalayas, but has spent most of her adult life in Lynchburg, Virginia at the foot of the Blue Ridge Mountains, which she calls "a beautiful spot for writing poetry and memoirs."

The editors are donating a portion of their proceeds to Food First (www.foodfirst.org), a non-profit education-for-action center committed to establishing food as a fundamental human right.

꿰

www.steeped.org